1857 AND PRINCE NARENDRAJIT

About the Editors

Shukhdeba Sharma Hanjabam (MSW, Ph.D.) is an Assistant Professor and was formerly Head of the Department of Social Work, Indira Gandhi National Tribal University, Regional Campus, Manipur, Kangpokpi District, Manipur. He completed his Ph.D. from the School of Social Work, Tata Institute of Social Sciences, Mumbai, and his post-doctoral from the University of Florida, USA. He can be contacted at <hanjabam@gmail.com>

Pukhrambam James Singh (MA, Ph.D.) is an Assistant Professor in the Department of Sankirtana, Manipur University of Culture (Government of Manipur), Imphal-East, Manipur, India. He can be contacted at <jamesmuc2019@gmail.com>

Moirangthem Tineshowri Devi (MSW, MPhil, Ph.D.) is Professor & Head in the Department of Social Work, Assam University, Silchar, Assam, India. She can be contacted at <moirangi@yahoo.com>

1857 AND PRINCE NARENDRAJIT
(Sana Chahi Ahum)

Edited by

Shukhdeba Sharma Hanjabam
Pukhrambam James Singh
Moirangthem Tineshowri Devi

Published for

INTELLECTUAL FORUM OF NORTH EAST

CONCEPT PUBLISHING COMPANY PVT. LTD.
NEW DELHI - 110059

ISBN: 978-93-5594-769-7

First Published 2024

Published and Printed by

Concept Since 1974

Concept Publishing Company Pvt. Ltd.
A/15-16, Commercial Block, Mohan Garden
New Delhi-110059 (India)
T: +91-11-41101460
E: publishing@conceptpub.com, *W*: www.conceptpub.com

Cataloging in Publication--Courtesy: D.K. Agencies (P) Ltd. <docinfo@dkagencies.com>

1857 and Price Narendrajit (Sana Chahi Ahum) / edited by Shukhdeba Sharma Hanjabam, Pukhrambam James Singh, Moirangthem Tineshowri Devi.

pages cm

Two papers translated from Manipuri and one from Bengali.

"Published for Intellectual Forum of North East."

"... some of the chapters in the volume were presented in the ICHR's sponsored two-day National Seminar on Prince Narendrajit/Ranjit Singh (Sana Chahi Ahum) the 1857 War of India's Independence organized by Manipur Seva Samiti; Intellectual Forum of North East-Manipur; North East India Habitat People Front, Assam; & hosted by Assam University, Silchar in December 2022 ..."--Foreword.

Includes bibliographical references and index.

ISBN 9789355947697

1. Narendrajit Singh, Prince, 1818- --Political activity--India--Assam. 2. Assam (India)--Politics and government--19th century. 3. India--History--Sepoy Rebellion, 1857-1858. I. Hanjabam, Shukhdeba Sharma, 1983- editor. II. Singh, Pukhrambam James, editor. III. Tineshowri Devi, M. (Moirangthem), editor. IV. Manipur Seva Samiti (Imphal, India), organizer. V. Intellectual Forum of North East India (Gauhati, India), organizer. VI. National Seminar on Prince Narendrajit/Ranjit Singh (Sana Chahi Ahum) the 1857 War of India's Independence (2022 : Silchar, India)

LCC DS485.A88A15 2024 | DDC 954.1620317 23

Dedicated To

AHEIBAM KOIRENG SINGH
(1979-2022)

ꯗꯣ. ꯔꯥꯖꯀꯨꯃꯥꯔ ꯔꯟꯖꯟ ꯁꯤꯡ
Dr. RAJKUMAR RANJAN SINGH
डॉ. राजकुमार रंजन सिंह

राज्य मंत्री
विदेश और शिक्षा मंत्रालय
भारत सरकार
MINISTER OF STATE
FOR EXTERNAL AFFAIRS
AND EDUCATION
GOVERNMENT OF INDIA

The 17th August, 2023.

Foreword

It is a moment of happiness for me when the editors requested me to write the foreword of the edited volume, "1857 and Prince Narendrajit (Sana Chahi Ahum)". I was told by the editors that some of the chapters in the volume were presented in the ICHR's sponsored Two-Day National Seminar on Prince Narendrajit/ Ranjit Singh (Sana Chahi Ahum) and the 1857 War of India's Independence organized by Manipur Seva Samiti; Intellectual Forum of North East-Manipur; North East India Habitat People Front, Assam; & hosted by Assam University, Silchar in December 2022, which I happen to grace as the Chief Guest of the Seminar.

It was on December 18, 1857, that the Bhartiya revolutionary sepoys fought the British Empire, particularly the Sylhet Light Infantry Regiment, in the Battle of Latu (Karimganj, Assam). The Battle of Latu shows the seed for the Indian War of Independence in North East India. It was after the battle of Binnacandy (January 12, 1858) that Prince Narendrajit was arrested from Manipur and exiled to Kalapani in 1858. I am fortunate to visit Mount Harriet in Kalapani on 26th Febuary, 2023 and pay my homage at the place where our Manipuri freedom fighters were imprisoned. We are immensely thankful to our Hon'ble Prime Minister, Shri Narendra Modi Ji and Hon'ble Union Home Minister, Shri Amit Shah Ji for such a great honour to our heroes by renaming Mt. Harriet of Andaman and Nicobar Island to Mount Manipur in recognition to Manipur's contribution to the Freedom Struggle.

Prince Narendrajit/Sana Chahi Ahum was a popular leader in the Barak Valley, particularly Cachar, erstwhile Kingdom of Tripura and Manipur. However, there is very little literature on the contribution of Prince Narendrajit and his revolutionary sepoys. There is a need for documents about him, the historic battle sites (Battle of Latu & Battle of Binnacandy), and the unsung heroes associated with 1857 in North East India. The contribution of North East India, particularly in the 1857 War of Independence, is being ignored by historians and policymakers. It is no doubt that few historians and individuals documented the events, but it remains unseen from the public domain even within the state where it happened. Thus, these important events remain unknown or unseen, and the contributions of our heroes who sacrificed for the motherland remain unsung. The academicians and other interested scholars in the region should lead the responsibility to document and tell such important events in our country.

Lastly, I congratulate the editors, contributors, and translators of the chapters for their important contribution to nation building through this edited volume.

Dr. Rajkumar Ranjan Singh

Azadi Ka Amrit Mahotsav
Office Address: Room No. 131-C, Shastri Bhawan, New Delhi-110 001
Tel. No. (O) +91-11-23070739, Email ID - ranjan.rk@sansad.nic.in, mosedu-rra@gov.in
Residence Address : 59, Lodhi Estate, New Delhi-110003
Tel. No. (R) : +91-11-21421137
G20

RAJKUMAR SAMARJIT SINGHA
Descendant of Rajkumar Narendraji Singh/
Prince Ranjit/Prince Sana Chahi Ahum
Place: Jaribon, Assam State, India

Message

It is a matter of elation and fully delighted me as great, great grandson of Narendrajit Singh (Sana Chahi Ahum) that the whole life career, his works, early life, young life, as administrator (Leibak Mapu) of Jaribond Leibak (Hailakandi, Assam, India) and participation in 1857 Indian War of Independence leading the local people against the British is going to publish in a book. We all know that the Manipuri people started to settle outside Manipur for various reasons, particularly in Assam, Tripura, Bangladesh, and Myanmar in the eighteenth century and nineteenth century.

I regret that the documentation and research on Prince Narendrajit have not been taken up at par with his contribution to the 1857 War. I am delighted to learn my beloved brother, local historian K. Swapan Singha of Hailakandi, Assam that the book on Prince Narendrajit is going to be published very soon.

I appreciate the efforts of the Editors and the chapter contributors associated with this excellent work and congratulate you from my core of heart. I hope this book will find out the facts and history of the 1858 War in Cachar and Assam.

R.K. Samarjit Singha
Rajkumar Samarjit Singha

RAJKUMAR DUSARI GOPAL SINGH
Descendant of Rajkumar Narendraji Singh/
Prince Ranjit/Prince Sana Chahi Ahum
Place: Imphal, Manipur State, India

Message

It gives me immense pleasure to share a message for the book, "1857 and Prince Narendrajit (Sana Chahi Ahum)", who led the 1857 War against the British Empire in Cachar and was exiled to Kalapani in 1858.

Despite his popularity among the public, very little is known in Manipur about Prince Sana Chahi Ahum, his contributions, patriotism, and dedication to the motherland. To fill the gap, Shri B. Kullachandra Sharma through the request from the descendants has written a biography on Prince Sana Chahi Ahum in Meiteilon. The recent addition to the literature of Prince Sana Chahi Ahum should be appreciated.

The celebration of "Azadi Ka Amrit Mahatsav" in the context of the 75th year of Indian Independence marks the rejuvenation of Prince Sana Chahi Ahum and hopefully, it will continue to do for the future generations.

We wish the book editors, contributors, and the publishers for their initiatives to highlight Prince Sana Chahi Ahum.

Rajkumar Dusari Gopal Singh

RAJKUMAR JITENDRAJIT SINGH
Descendant of Rajkumar Narendraji Singh/
Prince Ranjit/Prince Sana Chahi Ahum
Place: Agartala, Tripura State, India

Message

I am happy to learn that a book, "1857 and Prince Narendrajit (Sana Chahi Ahum)" on the life and contributions of Prince Narendrajit/Prince Ranjit who was popularly known as Prince Sana Chahi Ahum among the people of Assam, Tripura, and Manipur is being attempted.

We the descendants of Prince Sana Chahi Ahum residing in Agartala firmly believe that the contributions and sacrifices of Prince Sana Chahi Ahum and his followers in the 1857 India's War of Independence is now being acknowledged and rejuvenated for the future pillars of the Country.

The public memory of Prince Sana Chai Ahum is still fresh among the people and despite his exile to Kalapani, we believe that he would return someday. With that intention and belief, we have not conducted the last ceremony (*Saradha/Aroiba Leihul*) of him even today. We have preserved his belongings and prayed by making a temple in Agartala.

With the onset of Amrit Kaal of Indian Independence, Prince Sana Chahi Ahum should not only be remembered among the descendants, well-wishers, and researchers but it should be merged along with the glorious history of India and more particularly in the education system of India.

We the descendants congratulate the editors, chapter contributors, and those involved directly and indirectly in bringing out the book.

Rajkumar Jitendrajit Singh

Acknowledgements

We would like to start by appreciating and acknowledging our contributors for making valuable contributions in the form of book chapters.

We would like to acknowledge the support from the Indian Council of Historical Research, New Delhi for supporting the National Seminar on Prince Narendrajit/Ranjit Singh (Sana Chahi Ahum) and the 1857 War of India's Independence. Some of the Chapters of the volume were presented in the National Seminar. We thank the Editor of *Imphal Times*, Shri Rinkoo Khumukcham for the permission to reproduce the article, "Narendrajit Singh: The Unsung Hero of Manipur in the War of 1857" by Anandita Singh.

We are grateful to Dr. Aashish V. Bhave of the Centre for North East Studies (CNES), New Delhi, and Shri Swapnil Shermale of the Intellectual Forum of North East for their discussions on the book.

We acknowledge and appreciate Dr. Rajkumar Ranjan Singh, Hon'ble Minister of State for External Affairs and Education, Government of India for writing the foreword of the volume.

We also thank the descendants of Prince Narendrajit/Ranjit Singh (Sana Chahi Ahum), particularly Rajkumar Jitendrajit Singh of Agartala, Tripura; Rajkumar Samarjit Singha of Silchar, Assam; and Rajkumar Dusari Goral Singh of Imphal, Manipur for sharing their valuable and encouraging words for the book.

We are indebted to Koijam Swapan Singha for sharing the image of Prince Narendrajit/Ranjit Singh (Sana Chahi Ahum) and to Robin Wahengbam of R&V Arts House for painting/sketching the book cover.

We are also grateful to Prof. Shri Prakash Mani Tripathi, Hon'ble Vice-Chancellor, Indira Gandhi National Tribal University, Amarkantak; Prof. Rajive Mohan Pant, Hon'ble Vice-Chancellor, and Prof. Sajal Nag (Senior-most Prof. Assam University; Prof. Ganga Prasad Prasain, Hon'ble Vice-Chancellor, Tripura University; Prof. Naorem Lokendra Singh, Hon'ble Vice-Chancellor, Manipur University; Prof. Paonam Gunindro Singh, Hon'ble Vice-Chancellor, Manipur University of Culture; and Prof. N. Rajmuhon Singh, Hon'ble Vice-Chancellor, Dhanamanjuri University for their encouragements in completing the book. We are also grateful to Dr. Pradosh Kiran Nath, Registrar and faculty members, Ph.D. Scholars, and Master Students of Assam University.

We also would like to put on record our sincere appreciation to our colleagues and advisors of the Intellectual Forum of North East-Manipur; Manipur Seva Samiti and Seva Bharati, Manipur particularly Dr. Ch. Chandramani Singh, Shri M.M. Ashokan, Shri L. Jatra Singh, Shri Kh Rajen Singh, Shri S. Tarunkumar Sharma, Shri A. Dhanachandra Sharma, Shri Ganaraj Singh and Shri L. Bobby Singh, Shri Oinam Mahavir Singh, and Shri Elangbam Boysana Singh, Assistant Professor, Department of Sankirtana, Kha Manipuri Hindustani College, Kakching. We thank Shri Ngangom Khelemba, and Shri Lasiram Onilchandra Singh of DDK, Imphal for helping us in documenting the event of Sana Chahi Ahum.

We expressly owe our indebtedness to one and all who are associated in one way or the other in bringing out this book.

Editors

Contents

Contributors' Profile

Anandita Singh is a Researcher at the Centre for Northeast Studies, New Delhi. She has extensive study of socio-political & cultural dynamics of the pre-colonial & colonial period in East of Bharat.
Email: anandita.nec@gmail.com

B. Kulachandra Sharma is a renowned scholar of Manipur, who has extensively written on different aspects of Manipur.

Kakchingtabam Ruhinikumar Sharma is an Assistant Professor at the Department of History, Ideal Girls' College (Government of Manipur), Imphal East, Manipur.
Email: kruhinikumar@gmail.com

Koijam Swapan Singha is Vice President, Assam Manipuri Sahitya Parishad.
Email: swapansingha147@gmail.com

L. Birmangal Singha is former General Secretary, Manipuri Sahitya Parishad, Tripura.
Email: lbirmangal@gmail.com

Manidhan Singha is an Associate Professor at the Department of History, SS College, Government of Assam, Silchar, Assam.
Email: ymsingha@gmail.com

Moirangthem Tineshowri Devi is Professor & Head in the Department of Social Work, Assam University, Silchar, Assam.
Email: moirangi@yahoo.com

Natasha Elangbam is Head, Department of Mass Communication, Manipur University.
Email: natashaelangbam@gmail.com

Ph Ibotombi Sharma retired as Chief Translator from the High Court of Manipur.
Email: ibotombiphurailatpam@gmail.com

Pukhrambam James Singh is an Assistant Professor in the Department of Sankirtana, Manipur University of Culture, Imphal-East, Manipur.
Email: jamesmuc2019@gmail.com.

Rajkumar Jitendrajit Singh is one of the surviving direct descendants of Prince Narendrajit Singh (Sana Chahi Ahum), and a renowned Writer and Columnist based in Agartala, Tripura.

Sanjoy Das is Head of the Department of Computer Science, Indira Gandhi National Tribal University, Regional Campus, Manipur. **Email:** sdas.jnu@gmail.com

Shukhdeba Sharma Hanjabam is an Assistant Professor and was formerly Head of the Department of Social Work, Indira Gandhi National Tribal University, Regional Campus, Manipur, Kangpokpi District, Manipur.
Email: hanjabam@gmail.com

Sonia Wahengbam is an Assistant Professor at the Department of Mass Communication, Manipur University.
Email: soniawahm@gmail.com

Sougrakpam Dhamen Singh is an Assistant Professor at the Department of History, DM College of Arts, Dhanamanjuri University.
Email: dharmen.sougrakpam@gmail.com

Yumkhaibam Shyam Singh is an Associate Professor at the Department of History, Imphal College, Government of Manipur, Manipur.
Email: shyam.history@gmail.com

1
Introduction

Kakchingtabam Ruhinikumar Sharma, Shukhdeba Sharma Hanjabam and *Moirangthem Tineshowri Devi*

The whip and the bullet were freely used
For a whole hundred years.
Scurry off like the rascals you are
You Goras of the British army
You can parade to your hearts content
In the maidans of London!
Leave our land to us
You firangi devil!

Those words* express the hatred for *firangi*, and the British colonial masters echoed throughout India's national movement. Long before the organised nationalist political activity germinated, there had been at least fifty attempts against the *Company Raj* after the battle of Plassey in various parts of India. Because of the disjointed nature of being confined to certain places and regions and unable to escalate the cause and movement beyond their narrow territorial confines, the pre-1857 revolts and rebellions were dealt with and suppressed in an intense, violent and bloody manner by the *Raj*.

The mighty popular revolt that broke out in northern and central India precisely a hundred years after the battle of Plassey in

*Quoted from 1857 in Folk Songs, compiled by P.C. Joshi, 1994, p. 119,

1857 was the first in the history of Indian people against the British to break the regional frontier. The outbreak of 1857 was, in reality, a product of the accumulated grievances of the people against the company's administration.

Popular discontent had been gaining strength among the different sections of Indian society. It was this discontent which burst forth into a mighty popular movement. Peasants, artisans, and soldiers fought bravely against the foreign government, and their sacrifice constitute a brilliant chapter in the pages of Indian history.

Mangal Pandey hoisted the flag of rebellion on March 29, 1857. It became a full-fledged war when the military forces of Meerut cantonment raised the standard of rebellion on May 10, 1857. The sky was rent with the crush of *"Delhi Chalo"* and *"Maro Ferangi Ko"*. The event of 1857 became a prelude to the long drama of the epoch-making freedom movement that was to unfold in 1885 A.D. The causes of the movement are to be found in those hundred years of British rule in which the greased cartridges were the proverbial ignition that set the whole mine ablaze. The greased cartridge was merely the match that exploded the mine, which had, owing to several causes, been preparing for a long time. Various sections of the population felt suffocated under the tyranny of the foreign rulers, so they tried to free themselves from the foreign yoke. Freedom from foreign domination has been the yearning of all civilized people of every age, and the Indians were no exception. So, they raised the standard of revolt against British rule in 1857.

A considerable section of the princes, landed aristocracies, Chieftains, Talukdars, peasants, etc., lent to the 'mutiny' another hue. Rani Lakshmi Bai (Jhansi), Kunwar Singh, Umer Singh (Allahabad), Reza Ali Khan, Hyder Ali Khan (Rajgir), Jeodhur Singh (Bihar), Peer Ali Khan, Aosaf Hussein (Patna), Surendra Sahee (Sambulpur), Bishonath Sahee (Lohardaga), Arjoon Singh (Singhbhum), Neelmony Singh (Bankura), Bindabun Teewaree (Midnapore), Rao Bhopal Singh, Ahmad Khan (Multan), Mahtab Singh (Aligarh), Faniram Dutta (Assam), Man Singh (Shahagunge), Muhammad Bakht Khan (Rohtak), Muhammad Khan (Bijnor),

Prince Feroze Shah (Delhi), Raja of Satasi, Begum Hazrat Mahal (Rohilkhand), Muhammad Sasan (Gorakhpur), Hyder Ali Khan (Gaya), Subadar Ali Baksh (Hamirpur), Raja of Banpur, Raja Sankar Shah (Jubbulpore), Waris Ali (Patna), Nilambar and Pitambar Sahee (Palamau), Maulvi Sarfaraz Ali (Shahjehanpur), Muhammad Ahmadulla (Lucknow), Narpat Singh (Ruyia), Khan Bahadur Khan (Bareilly), Raja of Mitauli, Raja of Sel (Sitapur, Oudh), Rajas of Beapur and Shahgarh (Saugor and Narbadda Territories), Nana Saheb, Tantia Tope (hanged on April 18, 1859), Bakhtawar Khan, Jwala Prasad, Azimullah (Cawnpore), etc., etc., were some of a large number of other influential men who had participated in the great upheaval of 1857.

There has been a rich corpus of literature on this theme, drawing the attention of men of various shades of opinion on whether it was a munity or a national struggle.[1] The volume will not cover the details of the debates but focus on the perspective of a national struggle. The concept of "a national struggle", as articulated by V.D. Savarkar[2], Talmiz Khaldun, S.B. Chaudhuri and Promode Sengupta[3], to name a few. Chaudhuri Sashi Bhusan[4], in a pioneering work on civil disturbances before the mutiny, listed a large number of rebellions that preceded the mutiny. To see 1857 as a climax of such civil disturbances is to take a different position from the dominant British official version of it as a soldier's mutiny or as a feudal revolt in which the feudal classes took up arms against the British to protect their privileged position.

A close reading of the different sources reveals that it was not only the sepoys who rose in revolt; it was a combination of grievances, national hatred, and religious fanaticism against the English occupation of India. It remained a shining example before nascent nationalism in India in its struggle for freedom from the British yoke and was imbued with the full glory of the first national war of independence against the British. Why is it called the War of Independence? It was the result of widespread public reaction against the British. Each of the common people in several areas rose in arms. There was remarkable Hindu-Muslim unity.

Without popular support, the movement would not have spread so quickly; everywhere, *maro ferangee ko* was the familiar slogan. Apart from general social, economic, and political factors resulting from the gradual subordination of India under the British colonial dispensation, the loss of prestige and self-respect of the people was the primary motive that goaded people to fight against the *Firangi Raj*.

The north-eastern part of India, though remaining aloof from the theatres of the 1857 War of Independence owing to geographical bottlenecks, did not remain silent spectators to what their brethren were going through. In the Brahmaputra valley of undivided Assam, the bugle for independence was sounded by Maniram Barua, popularly known as Maniram Dewan, who harboured various grievances against the British and raised the standard of revolt. Maniram Barua and several co-conspirators were arrested, tried, and executed. Like Maniram, the standard of revolt at Cachar of Barak Valley was raised by Prince Narendrajit, also known as Ranjit, and Sana Chahi Ahum, son of deposed Manipur king Chourajit Singh, who took shelter at the Cachar Kingdom after being expelled from Manipur in 1813.

The British official reported him as the movement leader who marched to Cachar from Chittagong (now in Bangladesh). In 'Takhelei' (a textbook prescribed for Class V by the Tripura Madhya Shikshya Parisad), while describing the role of Sana Chahi Ahum in the movement, it is written:[5] "The prominent example of his (Sana Chahi Ahum) leadership quality was his capability of being the leader of the peoples of Cachar in the Revolt of 1857. In the revolt, he was the ringleader and provided proper guidelines for shelter, food, and traditional medical care. His presence also aroused a new zeal in those rebel sepoys."

The British officials were under constant surveillance for him and his brother, fearing that they might revolt against the British as well as against the Maharaja of Manipur. They were removed from Cachar on October 16, 1841, to Dacca and finally allowed to return on November 7, 1851. The Royal family connection of the Prince heightened the suspicion of British officials towards Prince Sana Chahi Ahum. McCulloch, the then Political Agent at Imphal, expressed[6]: "Shortly after the mutineers entered Cachar, they were joined by the Prince, Narendrajit Singh, who was at large." In his report, Captain Stewart (Superintendent of Cachar), who was actively involved in containing the mutiny led by Prince Narendrajit, mentioned: "(i) … On January 12, 1858, the mutineers with Narindrajit (*sic.* Wrong spelling for Narendrajit) Singh, the Prince of Manipur, and his followers came out of the jungle and entered a village to the west of Binnakandi. Immediately after their flight, a heavy engagement took place …. (ii) … In the same letter, he again expressed anxiety over the possible alliance between the mutineers and the rebel sepoys. On January 13, 1858, he intimated the actual involvement of the Manipuri Prince and his followers with mutineers."[7]

Following the battle of Binnacandi (Cachar), Prince Sana Chahi Ahum was severely injured, and his revolutionary sepoys were defeated. Subsequently, Prince Sana Chahi Ahum was arrested on his way to Manipur on January 25, 1858, and handed over to the British, who transported him to Life at Kalapani. The exploits of this man are yet to be recorded in the annals of India's War of Independence. The lopsided account of India's War of Independence needs to be revisited so that gaps in regional variations are filled up in the near future.

Considering this, this volume consists of eight chapters, including the Introduction. The translated works from Bengali and Meiteilon are also part of the volume. **The first chapter, 'Introduction' by Kakchingtabam Ruhinikumar Sharma, Shukhdeba Sharma Hanjabam and Moirangthem Tineshowri Devi,** provides the background for the Indian national movement and the resentment towards *Firangis*. It states that popular discontent had been gaining strength among different sections of Indian society. This discontent burst forth into a mighty popular movement. Without popular support, the movement would not have spread so quickly; *maro ferangee ko* was the common slogan everywhere. Apart from general social, economic, and political factors resulting from the gradual subordination of India under British colonial rule, the loss of prestige and self-respect of the people was the primary motivation that goaded people to fight against the *Firangi Raj*.The north-eastern part of India did not remain a silent spectator. In the Brahmaputra valley of undivided Assam, the bugle for independence was sounded by Maniram Barua, popularly known as Maniram Dewan. Like Maniram, the revolt at Cachar of Barak Valley was raised by Prince Narendrajit, also known as Ranjit, and Sana Chahi Ahum, son of deposed Manipur king Chourajit Singh, who took shelter in the Cachar Kingdom after being expelled from Manipur in 1813. Prince Sana Chahi Ahum was arrested on January 25, 1858, and transported to Life at Kalapani for waging war against the British Empire.

The second chapter, 'Prince Narendrajit: The Leader of The Indian War of Independence' by Rajkumar Jitendrajit Singh and translated from Bengali by Prof. Sanjoy Das and Natasha Elangbam, emphasizes the significant contributions made by Prince Narendrajit during India's First War of Independence in 1857 in North East India. Prince Narendrajit was quite popular and renowned in that region for his bravery and innovation in weaponry. During India's First War of Independence, the combined group of rebel soldiers and loyalists led by Prince Narendrajit headed towards Sylhet to attack the British North Eastern Frontier base headquarters at Sylhet. Later, a fierce battle occurred between January 15 and 25, 1858, in Jiri. Prince Narendrajit was wounded in the battle and taken prisoner to Manipur on Monday, January 25, 1858. He was charged with war against the British by leading the revolutionary sepoys and was found guilty and exiled to the Andaman Islands. Prince Narendrajit's life in Andaman and his life after Andaman are shrouded in mystery. This chapter highlights that the 175th year of Indian Independence is celebrated in various ways across India; exploring the revolutionary Prince Narendrajit is crucial.

The third chapter, 'Manipuri Prince Narendrajit Singh: A Hero of the First War of India's Independence by Yumkhaibam Shyam Singh', states that the first significant uprising of the Hindustanis (Indians) in 1857, also known as the First War of India's Independence, had a deep impact on the people of Cachar (now in Assam). It occurred when the Indian sepoys of Chittagong (a part of British India) rose with their followers (family members and freed prisoners) and marched towards Manipur. On their way to the princely kingdom, they fought the Battle of Latu (Karimganj, Assam), where Major R.P.V. Byng and some sepoys of the British army were killed. During the historic battle, these rebels called out many times to the Hindustani sepoys of the British army to join them and fight united to root out the British from the soil of India. After the battle, these freedom strugglers entered the British District of Cachar, where local people joined them under their leader—Narendrajit Singh (a Manipuri Prince of Cachar). Later, the joint rebels reorganized their force, mainly with the addition of Manipuris living in Cachar, and fought a defeated war against the British army at Binnacandi on January 12, 1858. In the battle, the Prince sustained a gunshot injury and, upon being arrested, was sent to the Andaman Islands by the British Government. For the significant role Narendrajit Singh played in the freedom struggle, he was recorded as one of its leaders.

The fourth chapter, 'Battle of Latu' by B. Kulachandra Sharma and translated from Manipuri by Ph Ibotombi Sharma and Sonia Wahengbam, discusses the Battle of Latu on December 18, 1857. This battle was notably the first Indian War of Independence initiated by the revolutionary sepoys in 1857 on the north-eastern border of India, opposing the colonial rule of the British East India Company. The chapter highlights Prince Narendrajit's significant contributions in defeating the colonial rulers at any cost. In the gunfight at Jiri, recognised as the last battlefront of the First Indian War of Independence, he displayed immense bravery, risking his own life. Prince Narendrajit dedicated his life to joining the First Indian War of Independence in 1857 from the north-eastern part of India, raising his voice against the colonial and 'divide and rule' policies of the British Empire, advocating for an independent Bharat.

The fifth chapter, 'Sana Chahi Ahum: A Leader of North East India during the First War of Indians Independence' by L. Birmangal Singha and translated from Manipuri by Sougrakpam Dharmen Singh and Pukhrambam James Singh, narrates the greatness of Prince Narendrajit (Sana Chahi Ahum) and his active involvement in the First War of India's Independence in 1857. Simultaneously, sepoys of Sylhet Light Infantry, under the instruction of Superintendent Captain Robert Stewart, engaged the Kuki tribe to confront the revolutionary sepoys. The Kuki scouts, tasked with collecting secret information, kept Captain Stewart informed about the movements of the revolutionary sepoys, capturing some alive and killing others. Witnessing the dire conditions of the revolutionary sepoys, Manipuri Prince Sana Chahi Ahum, who was settled in Cachar, landed a helping hand to them. Sana Chahi Ahum aimed to drive the British away from India and save Cachar. The chapter highlights that on December 18, 1857, the first battle between the revolutionary sepoys and the British took place, and the last battle occurred on January 12, 1858, at Binnacandy.

The sixth chapter, 'Prince Narendrajit Singh and the Narratives of the Revolt of 1857 in Barak Valley' by Manidhan Singha, underscores the significant roles played by Manipuri Prince Narendrajit Singh in organizing the dispersed and deviated sepoys who entered into Cachar during the troubled periods of the Revolt of 1857. Recent research indicates North East India was entwined with the rest of India in revolting against British rule. The chapter states that Prince Narendrajit Singh intended to obliterate anyone or anything representing the alien British and restore what he believed to be his ancestral domain, leveraging the angst and hatred of the revolutionary sepoys towards British rule. The events in Barak Valley during the uprisings of 1857, termed insignificant by historians, demand reevaluation and in-depth research into

Prince Narendrajit's significant contributions during the First War of Independence.

The seventh chapter, 'Early Life of Narendrajit Singha (Ranjit Singha/Sana Chahi Ahum) and 1857 First War of India's Independence' by Shri Koijam Swapan Singha, sheds light on Prince Narendrajit Singh's early life and his contributions during the First War of Independence of India in 1857. From 1852 to 1857, Prince Narendrajit secretly organized war preparations and provided war training to Manipuri youths in the Tripura kingdom. The chapter concludes by mentioning that Narendrajit Singha/ Sana Chahi Ahum/Ranjit Singh and other Manipuri princes led the revolutionary sepoy of the great war in North East India, particularly in Tripura, Cachar, and Manipur.

The eighth and concluding chapter, 'Narendrajit Singh: The Unsung Hero of Manipur in the War of 1857' by Anandita Singh, highlights Prince Narendrajit as an exceptional leader and patriot who believed in the brotherhood of Indians and recognized the power of patriotism. He mobilized people, inspired them, and led them to the rightful path to freedom. Unfortunately, Narendrajit Singh disappeared from British records after 1858. However, his name today is engraved in our history as one of the greatest freedom fighters. His relics, including royal cloth, garland, *Paduka* (Footwear), *Shankh* (Conch Shell) and a handwritten copy of *Bhagwad Gita*, have been preserved and revered by his descendant, Shri Birendrajit Singh, in Agartala, Tripura. These relics are displayed only once yearly on Narendrajit Singh's birth anniversary. The chapter concludes by emphasizing that it is not just the story of some unsung heroes; it is the legend of people whose names have been conveniently omitted from the documentation process and, thereby, from our history. The warriors of the 34th Native Infantry, the Lushai chiefs, and every individual who contributed to the freedom struggle are the spark of *Swaraj* that continues to light our lives today.

Notes

1. Norton, John Bruce (1857). *Rebellion in India*, Richardson Brothers, London; Raikes, Charles (1858), *Notes on the Revolt in the North-western Provinces of India*, Longman, London; Malleson & John Kale (1892), *Kaye's and Malleson's History of the Indian mutiny of 1857-58*, Allen, Waterloo; Kishorichand Mitra (1858), *The Mutinies, Government and the People,* Calcutta; See Chaudhuri, Sashi Bhusan (1955), *Civil Disturbances during the British Rule in India (1765-1857)*, World Press, Calcutta.
2. Savarkar, Vinayak Damodar (1909, 2014). *The Indian War of Independence of 1857*, Asian Educational Services, New Delhi.
3. Ghosh, Kali Charan (1960), *The Roll of Honour : Anecdotes of Indian Martyrs*, Vidya Bharati, Calcutta.
4. Chaudhuri, Sashi Bhusan (1955). *Civil Disturbances during the British Rule in India (1765-1857)*, World Press, Calcutta.
5. L. Taranikanta (2005). "Sana Chahi Ahum", in L. Birmangal & L. Kumar (eds.). *Takhelei. Tripura Madhyashikshya Parisad*, SCERT, Tripura, p. 20.
6. Yumkhaibam Shyam Singh (2019). "Sana Chahi Ahum and the Manipuris in 1857 Revolt", *The Sangai Express,* January 2, 2019 & January 7, 2019.
7. Subir Kar (2008). *1857 in North East India: A reconstruction from Folk and oral Sources.* Akansha Publishing House, N. Delhi, pp. 42, 67, 68. Cited in B. Kulachandra Sharma (2011), *Sana Chahi Ahum.* Dushri, Keishamthong, Imphal, p. 140.

2

Prince Narendrajit

The Leader of the Indian War of Independence

Rajkumar Jitendrajit Singh

(*Translated from Bengali by Prof. Sanjoy Das* and *Natasha Elangbam*)

Introduction

A lane in Agartala's Doleshwar Kalyani is named R.K. Narendrajit Sarani, in honour of the revolutionary figure—Rajkumar Narendrajit Singh, a prince of Manipur. On this path, some of the items that had been used by the prince are kept in a small temple in one of his descendant's houses. The temple is preserved as a memorial site of Prince Narendrajit.[1]

Prince Narendrajit was a prominent leader of the 1857 Indian War of Independence, in North East India. He was the son of Maharaja Chourjit Singh of Manipur. He was born at Sonai Mukh of Dunguripar, near Silchar. Maharaja Chourjit Singh left Manipur for Cachar as a result of the fraternal conflict in Manipur. The three brothers—Chourjit, Marjit, and Gambhir Singh, together dethroned and expelled the Cachar king, Raja Gobind Chandra and ruled over Cachar. The south-eastern part of Cachar was ruled by Maharaja Chourjit. The remaining parts of Cachar became the kingdoms of the two brothers—Marjit and Gambhir Singh. The capital of Maharaja Chourjit was Dunguripar, where Prince Narendrajit was born.

Maharaja Chourjit spent the last days of his life at Nabadwip around the year1828. Prince Narendrajit was only nine or ten years old then. Prince Narendrajit grew up in his relative's house in a place called Jabir Ban or Jafir Ban of Hailakandi. Another name of Prince Narendrajit is Ranjit Singh. But the name by which he is best known among the Manipuris is *Sana Chahi Ahum*. This Manipuri phrase roughly translates to 'Prince three years'. The popular belief is that the prince was conceived in his mother's womb for three years.[2]

Prince Narendrajit and 1857 War of Independence

During the first War of Indian Independence in 1857, three companies of the 34th British Infantry located at Chittagong revolted against the British on November 18 and the revolting soldiers started marching towards Sylhet via Tripura.[3] It was during the reign of Maharaja Ishan Chandra Manikya in Tripura. When the Maharaja of Tripura stopped them, they took the jungle route to reach Cachar. During this time, they met with Narendrajit and asked him to lead them. Prince Narendrajit was quite popular and famous in that region for his bravery and innovation in weaponry. Apart from weaponry, he was proficient in medicine, dance, *geet* (song), and *Mridanga* (drum). He knew Bengali and Hindi, apart from Manipuri.

Prince Narendrajit was about 38 years old when the rebel soldiers came to him. Among the mementos preserved in the temple of Doleshwar Kalyani is his *Janam Kushtia* (birth chart) along with other things. The *Janam Kushtia* is 17 feet long and according to it, he was born in Saka 1741, which corresponds to 1819 AD, on Tuesday, the second of *Sajibu*.[4] *Sajibu* is the first month of the year in the Meitei calendar. It starts early in *Chaitra* or end of March. So, the second day of Sajibu may be the 23rd of March.

Prince Narendrajit joined the rebels as he was against the British domination in the region. Maharaja Chourjit's Nabadwip settlement had been forced to succumb to the pressure of the British. Perhaps, Narendrajit feared that the British wanted to secure the throne of their ally, the King of Manipur and Chourjit's nephew, Maharaj Chandrakirti.[5] On his invitation, many Manipuris from Cachar joined him. They may not have been skilled in warfare but they were brave and loyal to Narendrajit. They were always ready to lay down their lives for him. This combined group of rebel soldiers and loyalists led by Prince Narendrajit headed towards Sylhet to attack the base headquarters of the British North Eastern Frontier at Sylhet.[6]

On the way, they had a fierce encounter with the British Light Infantry (later renamed 44 Native Infantry) at a place called 'Latu' on the border of Cachar-Sylhet. In this clash, a battalion commander of a British army, named Major Byng, was killed.[7] But Narendrajit's army could not survive the increasing attack of the strong British forces and many soldiers were killed and wounded. At that time, the British forces were led by Lieutenant Rose.[8] However, most of the dead were common people who were followers of Prince Narendrajit.[9] The army retreated and hid in the hills near Mohanpur. From there, they moved forward and looked for an opportunity to loot the treasury of Silchar. On hearing this news, a large British force from the British base at Badarpur moved to the hills of Mohanpur and surrounded it. Narendrajit's army and supporters were killed and injured in the subsequent battle. The battleground is known today as *Rana Tila*.[10]

With the remaining soldiers, Narendrajit marched east towards Manipur and reached the border of Cachar and Manipur's Jiri hill region. As soon as this news reached, the British Political Agent of Manipur, McCullum, he sought help from Maharaja Chandrakirti of Manipur to suppress the rebellion. The Maharaja sent six hundred soldiers under the command of Nameirakkapa.[11] In another description, the Maharaja sent four hundred riflemen led by Major Roma.[12] A fierce battle began with the Manipuri troops in the hills of Jiri. This battle took place between the 15th and 25th of January 1858.[13] Prince Narendrajit was wounded in the battle and taken prisoner to Manipur on Monday, the 25th of January, 1858.[14] Out of the remaining soldiers, many were wounded and killed. Many of the soldiers died in the mountains due to various diseases and starvation and many were captured.[15] At the request of the British government, Maharaja Chandrakirti handed over Narendrajit to the British authorities at Cachar. There, he was charged with waging war against the British for leading the 1857 Revolt. He was found guilty and sent to the Andaman Islands on the 28th day of *Sajibu, Saka* 1795, i.e., at the end of April, 1858.

Mystery of Prince Narendrajit

Prince Narendrajit's life in the Andamans and thereafter is shrouded in mystery. Did he complete his sentence in Andaman? Or did he disappear from there before completing his term? The answers to these questions are still not available. There are various legends about his life of this period. Some say that he did not return to mainland India after the expiry of his term. Some say that he escaped from the Andamans and went up to the Sundarbans. One version says a grateful Andaman Jailor helped Prince Narendrajit to escape as the prince had cured the Jailor's wife of a serious illness.

According to another belief, he was seen in various places of Cachar in the guise of a saint. His descendants still worship him. They believe that he did not die in the Andamans. Many believe that he was seen in a small mound in the middle of the Barak River of Phulertal. The place is now a centre of pilgrimage, popularly known as Nagoor Baba. It is believed that an old man called Sana Chahi Ahum is sometimes seen there. Whether he is a God or a man cannot be known but his waist is said to be bound by iron chains. Sometimes, he is seen crossing the river on bare feet or on a banana leaf. These are all legends. However, one thing that becomes clear is that the saintly form of Sana Chahi Ahum is even more popular than the historical rebel leader. But in the minds of the Jabi of Hailakandi, many places where Prince Narendrajit grew up are associated with his memory. The banyan tree on the banks of the Katakhal River, where the boat, loaded with his weapons, was tied, still stands today. The name of Sana Chahi Ahum still connotes to many an entity shrouded in fear, devotion, fascination, and mystery.

It is the right time now, when the 175th year of Indian Independence is being celebrated across India, to find out more about the revolutionary figure, Prince Narendrajit. It is necessary to determine which of the information about this multidimensional figure are factually true. Prince Narendrajit or Sana Chahi Ahum does not belong to the world of fairy tales or folklore. His true place among the heroes of India's First War of Independence (1857) needs to be evaluated and his contributions duly recognized.

Notes

1. The memorabilia preserved in Dhaleshwar Kalyani are (i) royal clothes, (ii) kharam, (iii) war clothes, (iv) nirgkhum, (v) mala, and (vi) ajjkaan, etc.
2. E.W. Dun, *Gazetteer of Manipur*, 1886, reprint, Vivek Publishing Company, New Delhi, 1981, p. 47.
3. Sri Shubhram Singha, *Poknafam*, is a Manipuri daily published from Silchar on 16 April, 2007.
4. *Maruup*, Manipuri Weekly, Agartala, 27 October, 2007.
5. Dr. (Smt.) Sobita Keisham, "Sana Chahi Ahum, The sepoy mutiny hero of Manipur", *Bulletin*, Vol. 1994, The Heritage Manipur, p. 32.
6. B. Kula Chandra Sharma, *Sana Chahi Ahum*, B. Rosan Manuscript Library, Imphal, 1998, 63.
7. *Tadev*, p. 72.
8. Dr. (Smt.) Sobita Keisham, *Tadev*, p. 34.
9. B. Kula Chandra Sharma, *Sana Chahi Ahum*, B. Rosan Manuscript Library, Imphal 1998, p. 72.
10. Sri Shubhram Singha, *Poknafam*, is a Manipuri daily published from Silchar on 16 April, 2007.
11. Chaitharul Kumbhaba Manipuri Sahitya Parishad, p. 335.
12. Dr. (Smt.) Sobita Keisham, "Sana Chahi Ahum, The sepoy mutiny hero of Manipur", *Bulletin,* Vol. 1994, The Heritage Manipur.
13. B. Kula Chandra Sharma, *Sana Chahi Ahum*, B. Rosan Manuscript Library, Imphal, 1998, p. 25.
14. Dr. (Smt.) Sobita Keisham, "Sana Chahi Ahum, The sepoy mutiny hero of Manipur", *Bulletin*, Vol. 1994, The Heritage Manipur.
15. E.W. Dun, *Gazetteer of Manipur, 1886*, reprint, Vivek Publishing Company, New Delhi, 1981, p. 47.

3

Manipuri Prince Narendrajit Singh

A Hero of The First War of India's Independence

Yumkhaibam Shyam Singh

The event of 1857, which was coined Sepoy Mutiny by colonial historians, was apparently the First War of India's Independence. In the event, the sepoys, who were Indian peasants in uniform, had a feeling of oneness among themselves without any tinge of caste, class, and religion. They were also supported by Indian Rajas and their followers. In this historic war, Manipuri Prince Narendrajit Singh/Sana Chahi Ahum/Ranjit Singh (a son of Maharaja Chourjit Singh of Manipur), who was born and brought up in Cachar (now in Assam), played a great role in taking sides with the rising sepoys of Chittagong (a British territory now in Bangladesh) who were on their way to Manipur with their family members and freed prisoners in December 1857. Narendrajit Singh and his followers' joining converted the uprising of Chittagong sepoys to a Peoples' War against the British Government. On his participation in the struggle, McCulloch, the then Political Agent at Imphal, expressed: "Shortly after the mutineers entered Cachar, they were joined by the Prince, Narendrojeet Sing who was at large."[1] But it is really unjust that this great man of the First War of India's Independence has not been given any space on the pages of the history of India. This chapter is an attempt to highlight the real contribution made by the prince in the said war so that his role can be placed in the historical perspective. The method followed is analytical with exploratory and interpretative approaches and the source materials are archival, secondary, and oral sources.

I

In 1813, Maharaja Chourjit Singh of Manipur was dethroned and then expelled from his kingdom by his brother Marjit Singh. The Maharaja and his brother Gambhir Singh, therefore, took shelter in Cachar. After living five years in the new place, the Manipuri brothers subsequently dethroned Raja Govindchandra of Cachar, and they became rulers of the valley from 1818 to 1823. On it, A.C. Banerjee wrote, "Towards the middle of the year 1818 the Cachar Raja was ousted from his kingdom and compelled to take shelter at Sylhet."[2] Consequently, Chourjit Singh ruled over the south-eastern part of Cachar making his capital at Dungurirpar near Sonaimukh.[3] It was during this period that Prince Narendrajit Singh was born on Tuesday, 27 April 1819, at Dunguripar, Sonaimukh in Cachar.[4] But the prince grew up in Jaribon (Hailakandi, South Cachar). By that time, South Cachar, being a British territory since 1832, became a hot spot for British economic and political activities. Consequently, the political life of Manipuri princes in Cachar was shattered into pieces degrading their social status and the honour they enjoyed before. Economically, the British tea planters created problems on land and the village life of the people of Cachar. It was also during this time—that Narendrajit Singh acquired the knowledge of firearms as his elders defended the Jaribon region against Kuki raids with the weapon.

By that time in Manipur, Raja Gambhir Singh died in 1834. Consequently, his infant son Chandrakirti Singh became the Raja of Manipur with the support of Nur Singh (the Regent). But as the latter was a distant member of the ruling family, many Manipuri princes of Cachar revolted against the Government of Manipur. Consequently, Tribhubanjit Singh (brother of Narendrajit Singh) also revolted in May 1841 but was defeated and killed in Manipur.

After this event, it was heard in Manipur that three Manipuri princes of Cachar—Pabitra Singh, Khoiraba alias Neelumber and young Narendrajit Singh were hatching a conspiracy for another revolt against Manipur. Therefore, Mr. Gordon (Political Agent, Manipur) intimated Captain Lyons (Superintendent, Cachar) to arrest the three princes and placed them in confinement.[5] The Superintendent of Cachar, therefore, arrested them on 16 October, 1841, and they were removed to Dacca. On it, a record accounts, "H.L in Cl. (His Lordship in Council) is of the opinion that the persons, Parbittar Sing, Khoiraba Singh, and the brother of the late Triboobanjeet (Narendrajit Singh), should be removed to Dacca and detained there under such precautionary surveillance as may prevent their return to the hills without the knowledge and sanction of Government."[6] As Narendrajit Singh had not done any harm directly towards the British Government, he submitted a petition on 25 April, 1842, with "complaints of being illegally imprisoned by the Superintendent of Cachar & solicits Government to direct his release."[7] But the prince's request was not considered. Later, at the request of Raja Chandrakirti Singh of Manipur, those three princes including Narendrajit Singh were released from Dacca by an order of 7 November, 1851. Hence, Narendrajit Singh was under surveillance at Tejgong, Dacca for about ten years.

This haughty disposition of the Superintendent of Cachar and the surveillance in Dacca made Narenrajit Singh a serious enemy of the British Goverment. On the other hand, the prince was exposed to the then Indian politics and also to the resources and capability of the British Indian Empire. It was ingrained in his mind—that until and unless a united Indian power confronted, the British rule in India would remain forever. Coming back to Cachar, Narendrajit Singh did not join the revolts against the Manipur of Leelumbar, Null, and Kanhai in 1852, and that of Wangkheirakpa, Kanhai, and Kishor Singh in 1856. It appears that, with a mature mind, Narendrajit Singh was waiting eagerly for the right moment to strike and expel the British Government from India in general and Cachar in particular.

II

At this juncture, the mutiny of sepoys inflamed Meerut and Delhi (May 1857) declaring Bahadur Shah Zafar as their king. Soon it turned into a violent Indian struggle in which Bakht Khan was the Commander-in-Chief of the rebel forces in the beginning. The unrest of the sepoys reverberated in Chittagong. Consequently, three companies of the 34th Native Infantry of the district mutinied on 18 November, 1857 and marched towards Dacca so that they could join the 73rd Native Infantry and drift united towards Delhi for a common cause against the British. But, as the road to Delhi was blocked by the British forces, they decided to march to the kingdom of Manipur. On the real motive of the sepoys of Chittagong, a special narrative of the Government of Bengal expressed: "Two of the mutineers were captured by the police of Noacolly and the villagers, on being interrogated, stated that on leaving Chittagong the detachment had intended to proceed to Delhi, but hearing that the road to the north-west had been closed by European, they were marching eastward with a view of reaching Munipoor, and obtaining the protection of the Rajah of that country."[8] Mr. Brenand, the then Principal of Dacca College, an eye witness of the incidents at Dacca, also noted in his diary on 29 November, 1857, "The Chittagong mutineers were on their way to Dacca, and it was supposed that their objective was to join the men of the seventy-third."[9]

After a long and tiresome march towards the north-east, the rebels fought the Battle of Latu (Karimganj, Assam) against the Sylhet Light Infantry Regiment (British army) on 18 December, 1857. In the battle, Major R.P.V. Byng and some sepoys of the British army were killed. When the Major was shot down, the rebels, with great emotions, called out to those Indian sepoys of the Sylhet Light Infantry, "Now we have killed the Sahib; come and join us."[10] These historic words also reveal that those rebel sepoys had a strong feeling of oneness of all the sepoys irrespective of the rebel or the British side.

After the battle, the rebels entered Cachar on 20 December, 1857, and they were joined by Narendrajit Singh and his party. At that time in Cachar, the report of the event of Latu was received on the late night of 19 December, 1857. Instantly, Manipuri princes viz., Sangie Thaba, Kunnai Sing, Mypha, Hawjaw, Khem Sing, and Khoirakpa were arrested by the British authorities. On it, W.J. Allan reported that these princes "suspected of hostile designs were arrested in December last by order of the officiating Superintendent as a precautionary measure when the mutineers of the 34th Native Infantry were marching in the Cachar District towards Munneepore."[11] But the British authorities of Cachar failed to arrest Narendrajit Singh. It is quite apparent that the prince was guiding those Chittagong rebels after the Battle of Latu. In fact, the rebels were divided into 3/4 groups and took Jungle routes in the Serespore Hills to evade the glimpse of Lt. Ross's party at Panchgan. They also passed the open field of Company Gunge at night without any hardship. Thereafter, they started a long march towards the Bhuban Hills where they could get a safe shelter and re-organize their fighting force. Since the large number of arms and ammunition was a heavy load on their long march, Narendrajit Singh shifted some of it to the Kalapahar (a hill in Hailakandi) using a boat which had taken the course of the Katakhal river. Then he concealed the loaded boat in the thick forest of the hill. An oral tradition of Jaribond (Hailakandi, Assam) also expressed:

> Narendrajit Singh fastened the boat loaded with arms at the trunk of a big banyan tree at the Kalapahar with a very heavy iron chain. The chain remained for many years firmly tied with the tree, but it was removed later by the staff of the Gagala Chherra Tea Garden. Sometimes at night when the weather was bad, the area, where the boat was hidden, produced an unusual sound like a paddler on a *Khurum* (wooden slipper).[12]

This aged and historic banyan tree fell down around 2005 A.D., and its long trunk, nearly 50ft. long, had a decayed look when it was visited on 20 November, 2009. The place, where this banyan grew, is now worshipped by the people of Jaribond.

In their long and terror-stricken march to the Bhuban Hills, the mutineers led by Narendrajit Singh and his followers successfully passed through historic places like—Serespore Hills, Companegunge, Mohunpoor, Jalinga, Chuttla Howar, and Bunderaj. It appears that the followers of Narendrajit Singh assisted the rebels with unstinted dedication. They arranged food and shelter for the cold winter needed by the families of the sepoys.

Above this, Narendrajit Singh also hatched a conspiracy with the staff of Cachar Jail for the escape of those arrested six Manipuri princes as their presence in the rebel camp was highly necessary for the latter's success. On it, Robert Stewart expressed, "Roma Sing (Longjamba Loma), the Dewan of the Rajah of Manipur, then in Cachar, had warned me that on a certain day, they would all make their escape and join the mutineers."[13] This warning came true as they escaped on the evening of 10 January, 1858. But, those six princes failed to join the rebel camp. The Superintendent, in the meantime, sent police parties to all the neighbouring Manipuri villages at night but failed to re-arrest them. As the nature of the escape was highly suspicious, the Superintendent took up punishing steps as he reported:

> I found the jail Darogah guilty of having allowed the prisoners to be outside the jail precincts after dark and sentenced him to suspension from employment for 6 months and I found the Burkandaz guilty of extreme neglect of duty in having quitted his charge and dismissed him.[14]

Later, on their escape, the officer also expressed, "I have little doubt but that it was pre-concerted."[15] It reveals that the prince had hatched a conspiracy for the escape of those princes. Possibly, Narendrajit also appealed to the people of Cachar to support the rebels and not to cooperate with the British Government. Therefore, when Stewart declared a reward of Rs. 100 for giving any clue leading to the arrest of any one of the six escaped princes, the people of Cachar remained silent. From the statement of the Superintendent, it is also apparent that the prince tried to influence 'the Hindusthanie sepoys' of the Sylhet Light Infantry to join the rebel camp.[16] Thus, Narendrajit Singh left no stone unturned to unite all the powers to expel the British from Cachar.

Although the rebels of Chittagong had a plan to enter Manipur, yet the prince did not consider it a good move as Raja Chandrakirti Singh of Manipur was a dependable ally of the British Government. The joint rebels, consequently, came out of Jungle on the morning of 12 January, 1858 for an attack against the British army. On it, a report expressed, "The mutineers joined by a Munnipoor Prince and his followers, came out of the jungles into a village to the west of Binnacandy yesterday morning at 10 O'clock."[17] After some time, a bloody gun battle started against the British army. Rebel women also took part in this battle as it was a question of life and death. The fierce battle continued for about two hours and the prince's party was beaten. On the war, another report expressed:

> The mutineers were beaten from home to home in the village they occupied. Seventeen dead were counted on the field among whom a Jemadar, two Sepoys taken prisoners, were shot, and one straggler of the retreating rebels killed by the scouts making a total of 20 killed besides the numbers who must have been badly wounded in the engagement. On our side, we lost 2 men killed and two badly wounded.[18]

On women casualties, Stewart reported, "Women (two badly wounded)."[19] Narendrajit Singh also sustained a serious gunshot injury. On 10 May, 1858, the Superintendent reported, "Dr. Shircore also deposes to having heard a Sepoy of the 34th N.I. mention his (Narendrajit Singh) name before execution, and describes the wound on his instep as a gunshot one, the Prince who joined being reported as wounded on the foot."[20] The battle of

Binnacandy was an epoch-making event in the history of North-east India. It made Cachar a historic place of the War of 1857.

After the battle of Binnacandi, Narendrajit Singh fled to the territory of Manipur with some sepoys, but they were arrested by the army of Manipur who were deployed there in support of the British Government. The army of Manipur then sent those arrested Chittagong sepoys to the British camp, but Narendrajit Singh was treated well and brought to the court of Manipur where the Raja also gave him a warm welcome. Maharaja Chandrakirti Singh intended to save the life of Narendrajit Singh by keeping him in the prison of Manipur. Therefore, when he was solicited repeatedly by McCulloch to send Narendrajit Singh to Cachar to face trial, the Raja expressed, "Although what the Sahib says—send in this brother of yours Narendrajeet Singh—is right, still he is my brother. I apprehend him for having offended against the Sahib-Lok (the British)."[21] This pertinent statement of the Raja confirms that Narendrajit Singh was one of the great leaders of India's struggle for independence.

But later, when Raja Chandrakirti Singh knew the popularity of Narendrajit Singh gaining day by day, he felt insecure in his position. Therefore, the Raja sent his cousin to the British authorities in Cachar. On it, a report also expressed that "against the pressing solicitations of his numerous relatives, and of a large party of officers and others in favour of detaining him in the country, the Raja ordered Narendrajit Singh to be removed to Cachar for delivery to the officiating Superintendent."[22] After Narendrajit Singh's disposal to British authorities in Cachar, Raja Chandrakriti Singh expressed, "As the British Government has been pleased to approve of my previous conduct I earnestly hope that in consideration for me the British Government even if his fault be found a heavy one may spare his life."[23] As the Raja was in good terms with the British, his request was considered. Therefore, on 10 May, 1858, Stewart expressed to the Government, "I am of opinion that it would be inexpedient to sentence this prisoner capitally—But would recommend his confinement for life as a state prisoner."[24]

As the prince was highly popular in Cachar, the Superintendent did not like him to detain over for a long time. Therefore, Narendrajit Singh was sent to Calcutta without any proper order from the Government as the Superintendent also reported:

> I have taken the advantage of a large batch of prisoners proceeding to Calcutta under a strong guard and have forwarded Norindrajeet Sing along with them. His presence and that of the other princes in Cachar is not calculated to allay the excitement which had recently prevailed among the Monipoories, and I trust that his honour will approve of the step I have taken, instead of awaiting orders upon a reference.[25]

Narendrajit Singh was, therefore, delivered to the Magistrate of Alipore, Calcutta. Thereafter, the Supreme Government issued an order which expressed, "Narendrajit Singh having been tried under Act No. XIV, of 1857, and having apparently been found guilty of a criminal offence ought not to be treated as a state prisoner...If imprisoned for life, it can only be the transportation beyond seas."[26] Thus, the prince was sent beyond the seas just like other Indian leaders of the war.

III

The objective of Narendrajit Singh in the uprising was apparently the expulsion of the British from India in general and Cachar in particular. On 17 February, 1858, R. Stewart reported:

> It must not be forgotten either that Munnipooris were once the rulers of Cachar (1818 to 1823).... That this is borne in mind by them was fully revealed to me in the events which have recently taken place. When the mutineers of the 34th N.I. entered Cachar and their strength and intentions were unknown, the agitation amongst the Munnipoorie population was extreme, and the station (British Headquarters, Cachar) was threatened each day with attack. Notice of this design

> came to me so often and from such different quarters that I could not but feel assured of their truth to a certain extent, and the account given by a scout, who was a prisoner in the camp of the mutineers, when the Munnipoorie Prince, Norindrojeet Sing, joined the enemy, amply verifies my apprehension. This account was to the following effect. That after recruiting themselves at Luckipoor the mutineers joined by the Munnipoorie population who were all prepared to assist, and possibly by the Hindustanie sepoys among our own troops, should return to the station, loot the Treasury and the Magazine, and make themselves master of the country....[27]

This report verifies that Narendrajit Singh and his followers strongly supported those Chittagong freedom strugglers whose previous objective was to march to Delhi to build up a united struggle of the Indians for the removal of the British Raj from the soil of Bharat. The battle they fought at Binnakandy was indeed an important part of the struggle since the joint party determined to expel the British from India in general and Cachar in particular.

But, unfortunately, this great son of Cachar has so far not received due recognition from historians. On the Chittagong rebels and Prince Narendrajit Singh, Sir Edward Gait expressed, "They still headed for Manipur, and were joined by some Manipuri princes, pretenders to the Raj, with a few followers."[28] The same area was also studied by H.K. Barpujari and he stated, "After marching through the Jungles of Hill Tipperah they (Chittagong sepoys) entered into South-east corner of the district of Sylhet with the object of joining in Cachar Narendrajit, the pretender to the Manipur Raj, and his followers."[29] In fact these statements seem to have less relevance as Narendrajit Singh fought the Battle of Binnacandy which, as stated by the Raja of Manipur, was directly against the British. Indeed, Narendrajit Singh led the uprising of 1857 in Cachar hatching many conspiracies to expel the British from the region. Therefore, at the time of his arrest, it was reported,

"Narendrajit Singh a prince said to have been the chief of the conspirators was arrested."[30] Ultimately, the Manipuri prince was recorded as one of the leaders of the uprising giving the remark, "He joined the Chittagong mutineers with his followers."[31] But this hero of the First War of India's Independence has received scant notice.

Notes

1. National Archives of India (hereafter NAI), Foreign Political Consultations (hereafter FPC), 12 August, 1859, Nos. 127-28, McCulloch to R. Simson, Munnipore, 7 July, 1859.
2. Banerjee, A.C., *The Eastern Frontier of British India*, Calcutta, 1964, p. 214.
3. Sen, Gouri, *Life in Kachari Kingdom at Khaspur*, Silchar, 2003, p. 41.
4. Sharma, B.K., *Sana-Chahi-Ahum* (*Ranajit/Narendrajit Singh*), in Manipuri, Imphal, 2011, p. 6.
5. NAI, FPC, 25 October, 1841, No. 84.
6. NAI, FPC, 25 October, 1841, No. 85.
7. NAI, Foreign 1842 Department, Political letters to the Secretary of State, Consultations, 16 November, 1842, No. 35.
8. West Bengal State Archives (hereafter WBSA), Judicial Department, 22 January, 1858, Special Narrative, No. 3, Government of Bengal.
9. Quoted in Subir Kar, *1857 in North East*, Akansha Publishing House, New Delhi, 2008, p. 153.
10. Lt. Col. H.J. Huxford, *History of the 8th Gurkha Rifles*, The Army Press, Dehra Dun, 1965, p. 17.
11. NAI, Home Public (hereafter HP), 14 May, 1858, Nos. 14-16.
12. Interview with Laishram Taranikanta Sing, D.D.K. Silchar, Dated, Silchar, 20 November, 2009.
13. NAI, HP, 14 May, 1858, Nos. 14-16.
14. *Ibid.*
15. Manipur State Archives (hereafter MSA), Stewart to Secretary, Government of Bengal (hereafter GB), Cachar, Dated, 10 May, 1857.
16. Choudhury, Sujit (ed.), *The Mutiny Period in Cachar*, Silchar, 1981, p. 43.
17. *Ibid.*, p. 19.
18. NAI, HP, 12 February, 1858, Nos. 55-56, also cited in Choudhury Sujit, (ed.), *op. cit.*, p. 20.

19. Choudhury, Sujit, (ed.), *op. cit.*, p. 27.
20. MSA, Stewart to Secretary, GB, Cachar, Dated, 10 May, 1858.
21. NAI, FPC, 11 June, 1858, No. 109.
22. MSA, McCulloch to Secretary, Government of India (hereafter GI), Foreign Department, No. 37, Dated, Muneepore, 17 April, 1858.
23. *Ibid.*
24. MSA, Stewart to Secretary, GB, No. 113, Cachar, Dated, 10 May, 1858, para 5.
25. *Ibid.*, para 6.
26. MSA, Secretary, GI to Secretary, GB, No. 2272, 25 June, 1858.
27. Stewart's report, 17 February, 1858, para 8, cited in Choudhury, S, (ed.), *op. cit.*, pp. 42-43.
28. Gait, E.A., *A History of Assam*, Delhi, 2003, p. 379.
29. Barpujari, H.K., *Assam in the Days of the Company (1826-1858)*, Gauhati, 1980, p. 193.
30. NAI, FPC, 28 May, 1858, No. 139.
31. NAI, Foreign Secret Consultations, 30 April, 1858, No. 362.

4
Battle of Latu*

B. Kulachandra Sharma

(*Translated from Manipuri by*
Ph Ibotombi Sharma and *Sonia Wahengbam*)

Following an order from the commissioner of Sylhet district, Major Byng of Sylhet Light Infantry arrived at Pratapgarh on December 17, 1857, covering a distance of 80 miles from Sylhet with a powerful troop. However, there was no trace or whereabouts of the revolutionary sepoys who had been ordered to be captured or killed. Major Byng intelligently gathered information and clues about the revolutionary sepoys and alerted his soldiers. After receiving reliable information, he proceeded with his troops towards Latu, located to the north-east of Pratapgarh at a distance of 20 miles from Pratapgarh. The British sepoys and Sylhet Light Infantry troops might have arrived at Latu simultaneously. The British soldiers were in hot pursuit of the revolutionary sepoys in Latu.

The Conflict at Latu

The revolutionary sepoys proceeded on foot for three days and arrived at the village called "Khan Bahadur Para", situated east

---

*Extracts from the Book, B. Kulachandra Sharma (2011). *Sana Chahi Ahum (in Meiteilon),* Dushri, Keishamthong, Imphal.

of Latu. They took shelter at the house of one of the *Nabab Mia*, who was the *zamindar* of the village, had food, and at dusk on the same day of their arrival, they moved on towards Latu and found the house of a Muslim *zamindar* called Kalamia, where they took shelter. However, Kalamia turned out to be treacherous and informed the British soldiers of their whereabouts, conspiring for their arrest. It was reported as:

> "Early morning, they arrived at Latu and searched for the Muslim zamindar Kalamia. However, this Muslim *zamindar* played the traitor. He received them in his house with false cordiality, but he secretly went to the riverside and found the sepoys of the British force who were searching for the fugitives. He informed them of the arrival of the mutineers and bargained for his loyal service".
>
> "The sepoys hurriedly reached Kalamia's house, observing the mutineers' number and position from a distance and rushed to inform the authority. When the traitor tried to entrap and arrest them secretly, the helpless mother fervently appealed to the Almighty Allah for redress. Suddenly, a terrible storm came down and ruined the house of Kalamia. The fugitive took blessing from heaven and managed to escape from the grips of Kalamia and took refuge in the deep jungles of Malegarh hillock" (*Ibid.*, 61-62).

Those revolutionary sepoys who had escaped from Kalamia's treacherous plan and found sanctuary in the dense jungle of Malegarh were joined by other revolutionary sepoys, including Manipuri sepoys hiding in various places in Latu. They realised that the Sylhet Light Infantry troops, under the command of Major Byng, were relentlessly pursuing them. They knew that a confrontation with the British East India Company soldiers was inevitable. Led by Subedar Ayodhya Singh, Havildar Rajbuly Khan (Meidingu), Rajkumar Narendrajit, they resolved to make the British soldiers understand that their sepoys, whether Hindus or Muslims, were all sons of Hindustan, united by the spirit of nationalism and unity, transcending religious differences. They holed up in the Malegarh jungles for a few hours.

The Confrontation

When the revolutionary sepoys saw no advance from the British army, they, along with the Meitei (Manipuri) sepoys, climbed up the Malegarh hillock, forming two groups under the command of Ayodhya Singh and Narendrajit Singh. They waited for orders to act. The Sylhet Light Infantry troops, led by Major Byng, realised that the revolutionary sepoys were holed up in the jungle and advanced. However, the revolutionary sepoys opened fire, and both sides engaged in a firefight. The news of the skirmish was reported as follows:

> "The British soldiers met the rebels near the Latu bazaar. Immediately, the mutineers took refuge on the top of the Malegarh hillock and fired upon the infantry. The British soldiers were disadvantaged, stationed on the riverbank below the hill. In the initial attack, Major Byng and five other soldiers from the Sylhet Light infantry lost their lives, and one more was seriously injured. Eventually, Subedar Ayodhya Singh's bravery enabled them to overcome the enemy. The mutineers then fled towards Cachar. In this encounter, twenty-six forces lost their lives." (*Ibid.*, 36).

The news of Major Byng's death reached Commissioner Allen at the Sylhet Headquarters. He promptly dispatched Lt. Ross of Sylhet Light Infantry with additional reinforcements to counter the sepoys. In the ensuing gunfight, British soldiers apprehended seventeen sepoys who were later tied to a large tree near the end of the Latu market and shot to death. This site still stands as a chilling reminder of the incident and is preserved as a memorial in Malegarh for posterity. This incident was reported as follows:

> "In this encounter, several sepoys met a martyr's death, and seventeen were arrested. To the east of the Latu marketplace, the seventeen captured sepoys were tied to a large tree and shot to death. They bravely embraced their glorious fate. This tree still stands as a witness to that tragic event. The graveyard Malegarh Tila bears the memory of commemorating this valiant outbreak" (*Ibid.*, 63). British officials reported the death toll as 26 and 30 (S.K.M., 2008: 36, 38). It seemed deliberate to emphasise the casualties primarily among the sepoys, many were untrained recruits or recently released from jail.

The battle of Latu on December 18, 1857, marked the first Indian War of Independence initiated by the revolutionary sepoys against the colonial rule of the British East India Company, occurring on the north-eastern border of India. The Sylhet Light Infantry troops concluded the battle at Latu after the sepoys fled the front lines and sought refuge in the dense jungle. The news of the battle of Latu reached Manipur within a week, prompting the treacherous political agent of the British Empire, Major William McCulloch, to urge Maharaj Chandrakriti to take precautions to safeguard Manipur's border. Consequently, 600 armed Manipuri sepoys were dispatched to guard the Jiribam border under the command of Major Melananda.

The sepoys, including Rajkumar Narendrajit Singh and other Manipuri sepoys, crossed Cachar and adjoining places one by one, finding shelter in the forest of Pargana Banraj. Simultaneously, the British army pursued them, blocking forest pathways to prevent their escape. The Superintendent of Cachar anticipated that the Manipuri sepoys would likely guide most of them to Paragna Banaraj since Manipur is predominantly populated the area. Lt. Ross of Sylhet Light Infantry had been dispatched with 100 soldiers to counter the revolutionary sepoys at Nagdin Gram Village. In the meantime, Rajkumar Narendrajit Singh designated Ayodhya as the leader of the revolutionary sepoys and devised a strategic plan to confront the British army on all fronts. On December 31, 1857, gunfire erupted from both sides. After a brief confrontation, they fled the battleground, crossed the Sonai River, and once again sought refuge in the dense forests of the Bhuvan hill ranges.

By the end of 1857 and the beginning of 1858, as the first War of Indian Independence began to subside across the Indian sub-continent, the entire western border of Manipur remained on high alert. Several Manipuri sepoys were deployed to prevent the defeated sepoys from the battles of Chittagong and Malegarh hill ranges of Latu from entering Manipur during Maharaj Chandrakirti's reign, who had sided with the British. The Bhuban hill ranges, bordering Cachar to the west, stretched for 40 miles or 64 kilometres, characterised by dense forests and ravines. Lt. Ross and Captain Stevens of Sylhet Light Infantry each led 100 soldiers, leaving no stone unturned to track down the sepoys hiding on the western side of the hill ranges.

On January 9, 1958, Gurkha sepoys of the British army climbed the hill and spotted the sepoys on the other side of the hill, opening fire. A fierce battle ensued for two hours. Afterwards, Narendrajit planned to save the sepoys from the advancing British soldiers by leading them to the Jiri river valley within Manipur's territory. He believed the British soldiers would not dare to enter Manipur as it was an independent kingdom. Guiding his followers, he crossed the Jiri River and found refuge in adjacent jungles. Meanwhile, Captain Stewart, the superintendent of Cachar, informed Mr. MacCulloch, the political agent in Manipur, to consult with the King of Manipur and send elite Manipuri sepoys to guard the forest ranges of Jiri. This was reported as follows:

> "Based on the report received from McCulloch, Stewart informed the authorities that the Rajah of Manipur has dispatched 400 men towards his frontier to give assistance and cut off the mutineers should they cross the border. His force has been placed under my order, and I have directed the Major commanding to confine his operation solely to the Munnipore territory." (*Ibid.*, 41).

The 400 soldiers mentioned were led by Longjamba Roma, who was promoted to Major and Head of Office in the Tributary Affairs. Earlier, 600 soldiers commanded by Nameirakpam Major Melanda were dispatched as additional reinforcement to assist Senapati Sanakhya Yaiskul Lakta, Nepra Selungba, Nandababa Leirikyengbam Hanjaba, Leihaothabam Gokul Thakur and others who were well-trained in warfare and commanded separate troops/ companies. After the confrontation at Bhuban hill ranges, the superintendent of Cachar falsely informed the King of Manipur that Rajkumars were conspiring to invade Manipur. Acting on this unfounded information, the frightened King of Manipur, Maharaj Chandrakirti, sent Longjamba Roma with his 400-strong soldiers to face them and protect the throne.

Confrontation at Jiri Forest

Major Longjamba Roma reported his arrival at Jiri to the superintendent of Cachar, Captain Stewart, accompanied by his 400 soldiers. It was reported, "Captain Stewart then directed the Major commanding the Manipuri force to deploy 100 sepoys at the river Jiri and Barak confluence. On January 12, 1858, the mutineers, led by Narendrajit Singh, the prince of Manipur, and his followers emerged from the jungles and entered a village west of Binnakandi in the morning. An intense battle ensued immediately."

The gunfight at Jiri began on the morning of January 13, 1858, and the exchange of fire continued for 2 hours. Approximately 200 sepoys from the British Sylhet Light Infantry troops faced around 400 Manipuri sepoys along with revolutionary sepoys, including Manipuri soldiers numbering around 200, in the battle (S.K., 2008: 40).

The revolutionary sepoys were inspired with renewed valour when Prince Narendrajit Singh displayed selfless service and true nationalism to defeat the colonial rulers at any cost. In the Jiri gunfight, regarded as the last battlefront of the First Indian War of Independence, he bravely fought, risking his own life. A bullet struck him, causing him to fall to the ground, and the advancing

Sylhet Light Infantry troops captured him. Helpless, the sepoys had to flee and seek refuge in nearby jungles. Not much was recorded in history about the injuries sustained by Prince Narendrajit due to the bullet wound. He dedicated his life to joining the First Indian War of Independence in 1857 from the north-eastern part of India, not out of a desire for personal glory or the Manipur throne, but to protest against the colonial and 'divide and rule' policies of the British Empire, advocating for an independent Bharat. In those days, many Indian patriots and Meiteis from Manipur who resisted British colonialism were arrested, tried, and later executed or shot to death. One record stated: "On January 24, 1858, the British killed several rebels and apprehended two of them in an encounter at Jalenga valley. These two were tried and sentenced to death after two days of detention. Stewart presided over the court, and the convicts were shot dead in his presence. (*Ibid.*, 45).

5

Sana Chahi Ahum

A Leader of North East India during the First War of India's Independence

L. Birmangal Singha

(*Translated from Manipuri by Sougrakpam Dhamen Singh* and *Pukhrambam James Singh*)

Introduction

The first War of India's Independence of 1857 spread to Northeast India. On November 18, 1857, under the leadership of Subedar Ayodhya Singh and Havildar Rajbuli Khan of the 34th Bengal Native Infantry Company led a revolt against the British. The rebel sepoys seized weapons, looted the treasury and even attacked and destroyed the British jail, freeing prisoners. They then headed towards Tripura with the stolen arms and a substantial sum of Rs. 2,78,267. Many princely states and *zamindars* across India supported this uprising. However, when the Tripura king refused to support them, the rebel sepoys crossed the challenging terrain of Tripura's hills and embarked on a journey to Sylhet. From there, they planned to proceed to Manipur through the Barak Valley. Some of the rebel sepoys hiding in an Agartala village were captured and handed over by the government of Tripura to the British in Kumilla, where they were subsequently executed.

The rebel sepoys encountered numerous challenges due to the geographical terrain, language barriers, and cultural differences. Under Superintendent Captain Robert Stewart's command, the Sylhet Light Infantry pursued the rebel sepoys. Stewart also enlisted the Kuki tribe to oppose the revolutionary sepoys, spreading rumours that they possessed vast wealth, including gold and silver. He even offered a reward of five rupees for capturing the rebel sepoys, dead or alive. Kuki scouts provided occasional information to Stewart about the movements of the rebel sepoys. Some were captured, and others were killed. Witnessing the dire situation of the rebel sepoys, Manipuri Prince Sana Chahi Ahum, who was residing in Cachar, came to their aid.

According to British records, Sana Chahi Ahum is identified as Rajkumar Narendrajit or Ranjit Singh. The rebel sepoys, aware of Sana Chahi Ahum's reputation for courage, sent one of their leaders, Subedar Ayodhya Singh, to establish contact with the Prince. In the first week of December, Sana Chahi Ahum and his followers convened with the rebel sepoys at Pratapnagar (Patharkandi).

Upon receiving the news of the Pratapnagar meeting, the British swiftly dispatched a company of Sylhet Light Infantry led by Major Bing. When the company reached Pratapnagar on December 16, 1857, the rebel sepoys departed for Latu. Undeterred, Major Bing and his troops pursued them to Latu. On December 18, 1857, the first battle between the rebel sepoys and the British took place. In this skirmish, Major Bing, five of his soldiers, and 30 rebel sepoys lost their lives. Under the leadership of Sana Chahi Ahum and Subedar Ayodhya Singh, the rebel sepoys then proceeded towards Manipur through the jungle.

Manipur and Cachar's Political Connections

To comprehend Sana Chahi Ahum's life in Cachar and his involvement in the 1857 war, it is essential to delve into the historical context of Manipur during that period. In 1798, Yubaraj Labanyachandra ascended the throne after Rajashree

Bhagyachandra's demise, which led to a fratricidal war for the throne among the princes.

Two years into his reign, Maharaj Labanyachandra lost his life at the hands of his younger brothers. In 1800, Madhuchandra, his younger brother, became the king of Manipur. To keep his brothers, Prince Chourjit and Marjit, under control, he appointed them as Yubaraj and Senapati. However, Chourjit was dissatisfied with his position and, with Marjit's help, revolted against and dethroned King Madhuchandra. Madhuchandra sought refuge with Krishnachandra, the king of Cachar, who was married to Queen Induprabha, Madhuchandra's daughter.

Chourjit assumed the throne of Manipur in 1803 and appointed his brother Marjit as Yubaraj and Senapati. Madhuchandra, with the support of his son-in-law Krishnachandra, tried to reclaim the throne in Manipur but was defeated in battle and lost his life.

Yubaraj Marjit later attempted to seize the throne and initially sought the assistance of the king of Cachar. When he received no aid, he turned to the king of Awa and successfully took the throne in 1813. However, this made Manipur dependent on Awa. The defeated king, Maharaj Chourjit, fled to Cachar.

However, the king of Cachar, Krishnachandra, and his queen, Induprabha, did not allow asylum to their uncle, Chourjit, who had killed their father. Helpless with no other way, he sought asylum in the kingdom of the Jayantiya king. After Marjit became the king of Manipur, as revenge for not helping him, he invaded Cachar in 1817.

At that time, the financial condition of the Cachar kingdom was in a mess, and they did not have the power to face invaders. To save the Cachar kingdom from the hands of King Marjit, Krishnachandra called former Maharaj Chourjit, who was taking refuge in the Jayantiya kingdom, to Cachar. The king promised to share half of Cachar with Chourjit if he could save the kingdom from Marjit. On hearing that his elder brother, Chourjit, would be the commander and his younger brother, Gambhir Singh, would be the Senapati in the war, Marjit returned to Manipur, turning his way midway. As agreed, the king of Cachar gave the southern part of his kingdom to Chourjit. He reigned as the king of Cachar, setting up his capital at Jaribond (Jhapirabandh) in the present-day district of Hailakandi.

Since the Burmese invasion of 1810, Manipur was under Burma, and Marjit did not want to be under the king of Burma. So, he fled to Cachar and took refuge in his elder brother's kingdom. The three brothers—Chourjit, Marjit, and Gambhir Singh—united by their common goal, expelled the king of Cachar, Gobindchandra, and divided the kingdom among themselves. The division of Cachar is quoted in the book 'Cachar de Itibriti' as

> "Cachar Raijya Eetipurbae Dui Angse Bibhakta Haiyashil, Akhyane Tin Angsabibhaktahael. Ae Samayhaite 1823 Prasanta Cachar Prithak Rajdhani Span Purbak Rajyasasan Karate Lagelan. Gambhir Singh Tilai Pahadre Pachimdic Prapta Haeye Sumarate, Marjit Singh Hailakandi Prapta Haoye Jhapirband Namak Stane Abang Sarjit (Chourjit) Singh Tilai Pahare Purbangsang Prapta Hueya Sonaimukh Niktabti Dungarpari Namak Sthana Raijya Karate Lagilen", (p.113) i.e.,

Gambhir Singh received the western regions of Tilain Hills and set up his capital at Surma. Marjit received the regions of Hailakandi, and Chourjit received the eastern regions of Tilain Hills and set up their capitals at Jaribond (Jhapiraband) and Dunguripara near Sonaimukh respectively.

In 1819, Chourjit shifted his capital to Dunguripara near Sonaimukh, where his third son, Sana Chahi Ahum, was born. Remarkably, he spent an extended three years in his mother's womb and was named Sana Chahi Ahum. His descendants, residing in Agartala, collected his Janma Kuthi and other relics, housing them in a temple where they are revered.

The Janma Kuthi records his birth as Ranjit Singh on the second day of *Baishak* (Tuesday) in 1741. In the Barak Valley, the birth anniversary of Sana Chahi Ahum was celebrated according to the English calendar on April 27. In Agartala, the descendants commemorate his birth on the second day of the Bangla month of *Baisakhi*. Sana Chahi Ahum grew up in Jaribon and had eleven siblings, and Rajkumar Tribhuvanjit was the eldest.

In 1823, Marjit and Gambhir conspired to expel their elder brother Chourjit from Cachar, taking control of his throne and property. Chourjit's appeal to the British for justice went unanswered, leading him to live an ascetic life in Nabadwip. The British provided him with a monthly pension until his passing in 1828.

The political landscape of Cachar and Manipur continued to shift rapidly. Gambhir Singh organized all the Manipuris settled in the Cachar kingdom and formed the Manipur levy. With British support, the Manipur levy, led by Gambhir Singh, marched towards Manipur, defeating the Burmese forces and reclaiming Manipur, including Kabow Valley, on December 28, 1826.

In 1830, unidentified assailants assassinated King Gobindchandra of Cachar. Subsequently, in 1832, the British annexed Cachar as there were no heirs to the throne. This led to the Manipur royal descendants who had settled in Cachar becoming dependent on the British. In Jaribon, a Manipur society with no monarchy, Maharaj Chourjit's eldest son, Tribhuvanjit, was appointed as the king.

Following the death of Maharaj Gambhir Singh in 1834, his two-year-old son, Chandrakirti, ascended the throne with Narasingh serving as his Regent. During this time, two of Chourjit's sons, Tribhuvanjit Singh and Ram Singh, launched an invasion of Manipur with 600 soldiers to claim the throne. On May 15, 1841, they briefly seized the Manipur palace, with Tribhuvanjit assuming the throne. However, they were defeated the next day in a battle against the king's army led by General Devendrajit.

Suspecting that the princes of Manipur in Cachar might invade Manipur, the British arrested Manipur's princes, including Sana Chahi Ahum, on May 16, 1841, and exiled them to Dhaka. During his 10-year stay in Dhaka, Sana Chahi Ahum learned Hindi,

Bengali, and other languages and gained knowledge of the British empire. He harboured resentment towards the British for their treatment of his father, Maharaj Chourjit, and desired to remove the British from India.

Sana Chahi Ahum and 1857

In 1857, upon learning of rebel sepoys of Chittagong entering Cachar through Sylhet, Sana Chahi Ahum allied with them, becoming a leader in the First War of India's Independence in North East India.

After the battle against the British army at Latur, the rebel sepoys, through a jungle trek, entered the borders of Manipur. The British army pursued them continuously. Since Sana Chahi Ahum was well acquainted with the terrain, he could quickly lead the rebel sepoys from one place to another. On December 22, 1857, while the rebel sepoys were resting atop a hill, they were attacked by the British army. Superintendent of Cachar Stewart said twelve rebel sepoys were killed in the battle. That hillock was later known as Rantila.

Regarding the incident, Stewart, in his report dated December 26, 1857, wrote:

> "On the evening of December 24, the British force led by Lt. Ross fought a battle with the mutinous sepoys. The British force attacked them while they seemed to be taking a rest after lunch. Leaving behind weapons, bags of rice, and money, they ran into the interiors of the hills."

December 26, 1857:

1. "… Lt. Ross again came upon the mutineers on the afternoon of the 24th in the valley of Jolinga.
2. The mutineers showed no fight but fled after the first volley. Our men, in pursuit, fired into their rear and killed several of them. In their flight, the enemies threw down several

> muskets, their bags of rice and rupees, and ran towards south-east escaping into the dense jungle in that direction".

To face the rebel sepoys, Stewart made numerous plans. A detached British force pursued them, and camps were set up in different places to fight the rebel sepoys. The British requested the king of Manipur, Maharaj Chandrakirti, to guard the borders. Stewart falsely reported to Maharaj Chandrakirti that the rebel sepoys led by Sana Chahi Ahum were approaching Manipur, intending to seize the throne. The king stationed around 400 soldiers under the command of Major Longjamba Roma Singh at Jiri to guard the borders.

After the battle at Rantila, the rebel sepoys led by Sana Chahi Ahum crossed Sonaimukh, Banraj, Govindanagar, and Kaptanpur and made their way towards the Bhuban hills. A British force fired on Sana Chahi Ahum and his rebel sepoys while crossing the Sonai River after he had made most of his sepoys cross the river to proceed to Bhuban Hills at Binakandi. According to Stewart, British soldiers were camping under Lt. Ross, Captain Stevens, and Lt. Binst at Binakandi and Lakhipur. The rebel sepoys also returned the fire. The volley of gunfire continued for about two hours, and seventeen rebel sepoys died.

In Stewart's report, two British soldiers died, and two others were seriously injured. Unable to face British soldiers firing under three British officers, the rebel sepoys led by Sana Chahi Ahum had to retreat. Through the jungle, they proceeded to Jiri, the area bordering Manipur and Cachar. They fought a battle against the Manipuri force led by Major Longjamba. Sana Chahi Ahum was arrested while seriously injured, and other rebel sepoys were handed over to the British.

Regarding the battle of January 1858 between the rebel sepoys led by Sana Chahi Ahum and the British, the January 13 report of Stewart mentions:

1. "… The Mutineer, joined by a Munnipoor Prince and his followers, came out of the jungles into a village to the west of Binnacandy yesterday morning at 10 O'clock.

2. Lt. Ross was stationed in Binnacandy with 100 men and Captain Stevens at Luckipoor, with the remainder of the force mounting to 150 of the latter, he had just dispatched 50 under Lt. Binst, at my request, to strengthen the Sudder Station.
3. While proceeding along the northern bank of the river, a short distance from Luckipoor, this party was fired upon by the mutineers from the opposite bank. Lt. Binst returned this fire, and the enemy engaged in front.
4. Lt. Ross then advanced from Binncandy along the southern bank of the river and attacked them right flank. Captain Stevens and Lt. Binst crossed the river in rafts under cover of this attack, which lasted two hours. The mutineers were beaten from house to house in the village they occupied and, at last, dispersed and fled back into the jungles to the south, pursued by our troops as long as it was practicable.
5. Seventeen dead were counted on the field, including a Jamadar. Two sepoys taken prisoner were shot, and the scouts killed one struggler of the retreating rebels, killing 20 besides numbers badly wounded in the engagement. We lost two men, and two were severely wounded."

The first battle between the rebel sepoys and the British was fought on December 18, 1857, and the last was fought on January 12, 1858, at Binakandi. In Stewart's report, during the 25th days of the 1857 War in North East India, 57 rebel sepoys were killed. The number of rebel sepoys executed and those who died of hunger were 229.

Maharaj Chandrakirti, the king of Manipur, honoured his brother Sana Chahi Ahum, who had been taken prisoner and seriously injured in the battle, and arranged for medical treatment. Chandrakirti knew that Sana Chahi Ahum never considered seizing the throne but aimed to push the British away from India and save Cachar.

The bringing of Sana Chahi Ahum as a prisoner of war to Manipur is mentioned in *Cheitharol Kumbaba* as follows:

> "11 ne (Phairen 25/1/1858)
> Ningthoukabada Mayambung Ebungo Chahi Ahum Mayangdagi Thungleiye" (p. 335).

Further, *Cheitharol Kumbaba* mentioned that it was Monday in the month of Fairen, on 15/04/1858, Sana Chahi Ahum was sent to Mayang (p. 336).

According to the records of *Cheitharol Kumbaba*, Sana Chahi Ahum came from the land of Mayang (Mayang in Manipuri means people from outside the state), stayed at the palace for three months, and returned to Mayang land. There was no mention of the enmity and fighting of the brothers. However, while handing over his elder brother to the British, Maharaj Chandrakirti requested to save his life. "As the British government has been pleased to approve of my previous conduct, I earnestly hope that in consideration for me, the British government, even if his fault be found a heavy one, may spare his life." (Letter from Major W. McCulloch, Agent of Manipore in the officiating Secy., Government of India, Foreign Department, Fort William, 12th February, 1858, No. 13. MSA).

Honouring the request of Maharaj Chandrakirti, the British, instead of execution, exiled Sana Chahi Ahum for life to Kalapani. Among those sent as exile to Kalapani, he was the first Manipuri. Then, Maharaj Kulachandra and 23 others were exiled at Kalapani as guilty of charges in the Anglo-Manipuri war of 1891 and kept in custody at Mt. Harriet island of Andaman. In 2021, Mt. Harriet was renamed Mt. Manipur in remembrance of Manipur's brave sons.

Agartala and Sana Chahi Ahum

A significant connection exists between Agartala and Sana Chahi Ahum, who led the 1857 War in North East India. Agartala's Dhaleshwar Kalyani Lane was named after revolutionary R.K. Narendrajit Singh. The Meitei knew the place as the Jaribon locality because most of those who settled there came from Jaribon (now Hailakandi). They were the descendants of Sana Chahi Ahum. They built a temple and worshipped the relics of Sana Chahi Ahum. On the second day of the Bengal month of *Baishakhi*, the temple doors were opened for one day and worshipped. The relics of Sana Chahi Ahum, such as the royal robes, sandals, war cloths, *Ningthol*, garland, *Achkan*, handwritten *Shri Mat Bhagawat*, conch, the 17th-foot-long Janma Kuthi and others are lodged in the temple area.

Notable individuals from Sana Chahi Ahum's lineage contributed to Tripura's literature and leadership. Kamala Rani, the daughter of Bhupendrajit (Angousana), the third son of Sana Chahi Ahum, was married to Jyotirinda Chandra (Brajanidhi), the youngest son of King Birchandra Manika. It is said that when Kamala Rani married at a young age, she cried and was consoled by giving oranges. Hence, the name Kamala Rani is derived from Komla (orange in Manipuri).

The family of Bhupendrajit shifted to Agartala, along with their daughters, and settled in Dhaleswar Kalyani. His eldest daughter, Thambalsana, who divorced her husband, came to Agartala along with Bhupendrajit. Thambalsana's son, Ningthoukhongjam Chandras has passed B.A., B.L. and became a district judge of the Tripura government. At that time, the state of Tripura was one single district. He was the founder and President of Manipuri Sahitya Parishad in Tripura, established in 1963. Noted litterateur of Tripura and President of Manipuri Sahitya Parishad, Tripura, Rajkumar Jitendrajit, and the first Mayor of Tripura Municipal Corporation, Dr. Prafullajit Singh, are descendants of Sana Chahi Ahum. Rajkumar Panchhamjit, a descendant of Sana Chahi Ahum, was an officer in the Publicity Department of the Tripura Government.

Sana Chahi Ahum's life is shrouded in mystery, with various oral stories about his exile and potential release from Kalapani. It is said that Sana Chahi Ahum treated and cured the Andaman jailor's wife, who was suffering from a severe illness, and the jailor was deeply satisfied and released him from Kalapani jail. Many people retold that they met Sana Chahi Ahum in different appearances in different places of Barak Valley. His descendants continue to honour his legacy to this day, even though the details of his demise remain unknown. His great-grandson Rajkumar Jitendrajit said that the descendants of Sana Chahi Ahum had not yet observed his 'Lanna Thouram'.

The descendants of Sana Chahi Ahum were settled at Agartala, Tripura.

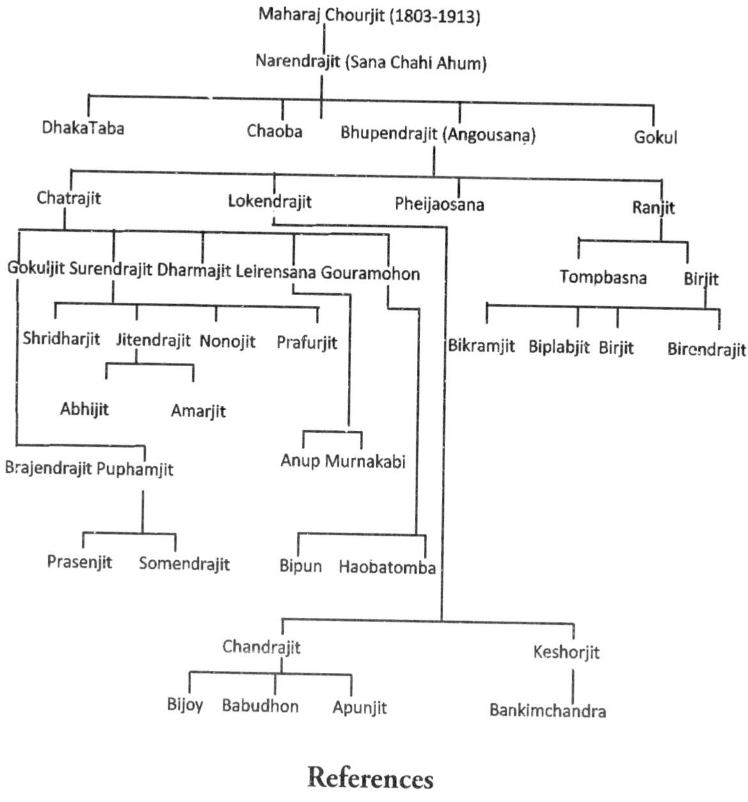

References

B. Kulachandra Sharma, *Sana Chahi Ahum*, 2011.

Gangumei Kabui Kamei, *History of Manipur*, Vol. 1 (Pre-Colonial period), National Publishing House.

L. Eboongohal Singh and N. Khelchandra Singh, Manipuri Sahitya Parishad, Imphal.

R.K. Jitendrajit Singh, *Narendrajit Sipahi Bidroharanayatam Neta*, Gomati

32, Bahur Sakho 2.

Sujit Chowdhury, *The Mutiny Period in Cachar*, Tagore Society for Cultural Integration, Silchar, 1981.

Upendrachandra Guha, *Cachar Itiribrata*, Sopan Publisher Sangkeran, 2012.

Y. Shyam Singh and N. Lokendra Singh, Prince Narendrajit Singh in 1857 Movement: Nature and Character from proceedings of North-East India History Association, 31st Session, 2010.

6

Prince Narendrajit Singh and the Narratives of the Revolt of 1857 in Barak Valley*

Manidhan Singha

The revolt of 1857 had deep imprints in the course of the history of India as a whole. However, history texts generally ascribe the geographical extent of the revolt as confined to northern and central India and it is said that the North East India remained unaffected by that event and its aftermath. Interestingly, some recent research has amply shown how the north-east India was caught up with the rest of India in reaction to British rule. The Barak Plains is relatively a remote area of British India, also echoed a serious outburst of the event of 1857; and had jeopardized the peace and tranquillity of the region at least for a period of two-three months. It is evident from the letter of Captain Stewart, Superintendent of Cachar, dated 16th January, 1858 which expresses his apprehensions of trouble due to the involvement of some Manipuri princes sheltering in the district, particularly Prince Narendrajit Singh. However, the happenings in Barak Valley during the uprisings of 1857 are being termed by historians as insignificant. But contemporary historians failed to pay enough attention to the actions that occurred throughout the valley during 1857-58.

---

*The paper is reproduced from *Southern Review* (2018), published by Assam College Teachers' Association, Cachar Zone, January.

Sir Edward Gait in his book, *A History of Assam* summarized the entire course of the event in three-four lines. R.C. Majumder hardly spared four or five lines on the issue of Barak Valley in his book *History of Freedom Movement in India,* Vol. 1 apparently. The opinion of both Gait and Majumder appears to be a reproduction of the contemporary accounts of the British officials. Dr. Jayanta Bhushan Bhattacharjee presented a seminar paper entitled *Mutiny in Cachar: A Survey of the Local Sources* and was published in the proceedings of North East India History Association, 1983. He tried to analyze a brief history of the happenings in the Cachar plains. But Dr. Bhattacharjee did not mention any role played by Prince Narendrajit Singh in the revolt. However, Dr. Subir Kar's book *1857 in the North East: A Reconstruction from Folk and Oral Sources,* New Delhi, 2008 gives a new light on the revolt of 1857 in Barak Valley. Dr. Kar basically tried to narrate the impacts of the events of 1857 in Cachar by taking a Bengali folksong material called Jangiyar Geet which prevailed in the valley. However, none of the so far discovered folksongs of Jangiyar Geet or any other, mention the involvement of Narendrajit Singh in the revolt.

However, there is no denial of the fact that Manipuri Prince Narendrajit Singh played a significant role in organizing the dispersed and deviated sepoys who entered into Cachar during the troubled periods of the Revolt of 1857. Letters from Major W. McCulloch, Political Agent, Manipur to the Officiating Secretary, Govt. of India, Fort William, Calcutta during the period indicates the involvement of Prince Narendrajit Singh. Further, Robert Brown, Political Agent, Manipur also mentioned the involvement of Manipuri Princes who were taking shelter in Barak Valley during the revolt. In the year 1982, The Tagore Society for Cultural Integration, Silchar, published the old manuscript *Mutiny Period in Cachar* edited by Sujit Choudhury, which is basically a compilation work of official dispatches of Captain Robert Stewart, the Superintendent of Cachar (1857-1858). Indeed, this manuscript belonged to the Late Robert Reid of England whose younger brother Mr. William Reid, handed over the manuscript to the Tagore Society. Incidentally, Robert and William are the sons of the Late James Reid, who was a tea garden manager in Cachar. The official dispatches of Captain Robert Stewart reveal the fact clearly that Narendrajit certainly played a vital role in the encounters which had taken place during the periods of revolt in the Barak plains. Therefore, any fresh revelation about Prince Narendrajit Singh and his times will certainly help to draw a full-length picture of the happenings in Barak Valley during the Revolt of 1857.

Prince Narendrajit Singh was the son of the deposed Manipur's Maharaja Chourajit Singh. Prince Narendrajit Singh was born at Dungripar near Sonaimukh in the present Cachar district in the year 1818 when his father, King Chourjit Singh took shelter in Cachar during the Burmese invasion of Manipur. Prince Narendrajit Singh was popularly known to the Manipuris as Sana-Chahi-Ahum. In Manipuri, 'Sana' denotes prince or one who belongs to the royal family, and 'chahi-ahum' means three years. It might mean that he was supposed to have been three years in his mother's womb. Interestingly, there are a number of popular legends in Barak Valley Manipuri society relating to the charismatic character of Prince Narendrajit Singh. Actually, King Chourjit Singh had left two sons Tribhubanjit Singh and Narendrajit Singh in Cachar. It is a fact that Barak Valley has had a close relationship with Manipur since time immemorial. Being a neighbouring kingdom, it had close political cultural, and trade affairs with Cachar. Therefore, scholars often remark that, without the history of Manipur, writing the history of Barak Valley remains incomplete. In the olden days, Barak Valley was the place of shelter for the Manipuris, a preparatory ground for revolt against the throne. As per provisions of the Treaty of Yandaboo 1826, Gambhir Singh, the younger brother of Chourjit Singh was vested as a sovereign ruler of Manipur, which practically, buried Chourjit's hope to regain the throne of Manipur. Seeing no hope, he at last gave up his long-cherished goal and left for Nabadwip for good. But his two sons remained at Jaffirbond in Hailakandi and they took up the unfulfilled venture of their father. In 1841, Tribhubanjit and Narendajit marched to Manipur and attacked on the capital. But they were defeated by Sylhet Light Infantry.

Tribhubanjit was killed on the battlefield. Thus, it is quite evident from this, that the crisis over the throne of Manipur remained one of the most volatile political issues of the region even after the restoration of the native rules to the throne. On the occasion of every change of ruler in Manipur, the rival princes were compelled to take shelter in Barak Valley. The valley became the political asylum for the Manipuris in those days. The Company authorities were also quite aware of the fact and tackled the problems by keeping strict vigilance on their movements and preventing their entry into Manipur. All these intricate matters created serious problems for the Company authorities in Cachar. Surprisingly, by the year 1850, there were not less than a dozen of Manipuri princes in Cachar who were constantly looking for an opportunity to capture the throne of Manipur. Among these princes Narendrajit alias Sana-Chahi-Ahum was the most capable. After the failure in his mission to capture the throne of Manipur in 1841, Narendrajit Singh returned to Cachar and settled in the Jaffirbond area (Hailakandi), where his descendants are still residing in many villages of the district. It is also known that some of the descendants of Narendrajit Singh are still living in Agartala. Prince Narendrajit Singh had a dream to become the king of Manipur. He was constantly looking for an opportunity to wage war against King Chandrakirti Singh who ruled as king of Manipur under the protectorate of East India Company.

On 10 May, 1857, the rebel sepoys of the cantonment of Meerut revolted. The District Superintendent of Cachar, Captain R. Stewart on 10th June, 1857 reported that the popular mind in Cachar was in no way affected by the reovolt which was occurring in the north-east. But by the end of the year, his assumption proved wrong. Capt. Stewart's report to the Secretary, Government of Bengal on 7th December, 1857 reveals an alarming change in the situation in Barak Valley. He detailed about the precautionary measures which had been taken to check the inroads of the mutineers sepoys in Cachar. In the same letter, he also expressed his apprehensions that the presence of anti-loyalist Manipuri princes in the valley and the Lushai chiefs in the southern part, who were at war with the British, rendered the situation more serious.

The 34h Native Infantry at Chittagong revolted suddenly on 18th November, 1857. The Commissioner of the Regiment failed to control the situation. The rebel sepoys plundered the treasury, released the covets of the jail, burnt down the barrack, looted the armoury, and flew towards Tripura. The Raja of Tripura, to show his allegiance to the British, sent a large force to resist the rebels. The rebel sepoys suffered terribly. Three elephants and a sum of about ten thousand rupees were captured from them. The dejected rebel sepoys then rushed towards Manipur through Sylhet. The rebel sepoys about 300 in number, reached at Langla in Sylhet district and they collected foodgrains from a Zamindar named Ghous Ali Khan. As soon as the news of the coming of the rebel sepoys was received by B.C. Allen, the Commissioner of Sylhet, he sent Major Byng the Commandant of the Sylhet Light Infantry towards Pratapgarh, sixty miles away from the Sylhet Sadar Station with a force of 160 army to intercept the rebel sepoys. In the meantime, anticipating the presence of the British force, the rebel sepoys changed their direction and following the foothills of the Patharia range reached Latu (Malegarh near Karimganj) on 18th December. Major Byng and his troops encountered the rebel sepoys at Latu for several hours. Major Byng was killed by the rebel sepoys. However, Subedar Ayoddha Singh of Sylhet Light Infantry ultimately succeeded to defeat the sepoys. A.C. Choudhury mentioned that the sepoys were about 300 in number in the Latu battle. In this context, an interesting observation of L.W. Shakespear's *History of Assam Rifles* can be taken into consideration.

The chief disturbance in the fifties which touched Chittagong and the Surma Valley was connected with the 1857 War, though fortunately only to a small extent viz. when the 34th N.I. revolted at Chittagong in November 1857, and marched northwards through Sylhet and Cachar hoping to raise those districts against the British which they failed. Engaged and defeated at Latu in Sylhet by Sylhet Light Infantry they were pursued to Cachar, where the S.L.I. joined by a detachment of the North Cachar Hills F.P. broke up the rebel sepoys in an action near Lakhimpur (*sic*. Lakhipur), where they fled into the hills across the Barak river, where Manipuri troops rounded most of them up and handed them over to the civil authorities at Silchar. It is said that, though the authority is not definite, that, the Tangal General (*sic*. Thangal), an old man who with the Senapati was hanged for the Manipur Rebellion in 1891, was of the 34th N.I. who escaped and took the service in that state.

The above-mentioned information invites a fresh inquisitiveness into the matter. After the defeat in the battle of Latu, the rebel sepoys escaped and scattered in groups. On the 19th December, Captain Stewart received a letter from the Daroga of Latu that the rebel sepoys had passed Deuliabond on the night of 19th December, and from there they marched towards Sirispur in Hailakandi, On December 21, Lt. Ross from Panchgram, who was given the charge to intercept the rebels, informed Captain Stewart that the rebel sepoys were split into three to four groups and all were trying to enter into Manipur. Lt. Ross rushed with 50 numbers of army men and 25 Kuki Scouts. He marched towards Mohonpur and intercepted the rebels. The hilltop, where the encounter had taken place between the rebel sepoys and the British force, is popularly known as Rantilla by the local people. Lt. Ross and the volunteer of Cachar Tea Company followed the rebels and about two dozen of sepoys were killed at Mohonpur. Perhaps at that point in time, Narendrajit Singh who was somewhere in Hailakandi district had made contact with the rebel sepoys. Possibly, he could suddenly realize that the arrival of the rebel sepoys in Barak Valley would be a good opportunity to make a fresh campaign to Manipur which was in the protection of the British.

In the course of time, a number of pitch battles were fought between the rebel sepoys and the British forces at Chatlahaur, Jalenga, Nagdirgram, etc. The rebel sepoys were defeated by the British forces in various places and some fled into the jungles to take shelter among the independent Kuki Chiefs of the Lushai hills. But owing to their good relationship with the British, the tribal chiefs did not entertain the rebels and handed them over to the British authorities of Cachar. Munjihow, a Kuki chief residing in south Manipur, assisted the British in capturing the rebel sepoys. On the other hand, Capt. Stewart arrested some Manipuri Princes of Cachar on suspicion on 26th December, 1857. He also reported that the Manipuri princes in Cachar were anxious to take hold of the opportunity to carry out their hidden desire to capture the throne of Manipur and Narendrajit became the spearhead. Therefore, even after the defeat of the rebel sepoys in the various places in the valley, the situation in the district was not free from danger for the British. All said and done after the joining of Narendrajit Singh, the rebel sepoys were re-energized and were organizing secretly to invade Manipur.

On the other hand, based on the report sent by Capt Stewart, Major McCulloch, the Political Agent of Manipur requested King Chandrakirti to send 400 soldiers towards the borders of Cachar to check the entry of the rebel sepoys to Manipur. In the meantime, on 12th January, 1858, in the morning Prince Narendraji Singh came out with his followers. He intended to loot the Cachar Treasury. But, at Binnakandi, he was resisted by a strong contingent of Capt. Stevens, Lt. Ross, and Lt. Binst from three fronts. After a long two hours of fighting, the rebels were defeated. In that engagement, Narendrajit received a bullet injury on his left foot. Subsequently, he escaped into the jungles of the Bhuban Hill. Thus, the battle of Binnakandi virtually washed away the last hope of the rebel sepoys to achieve their goal.

After the defeat in the battle of Binnakandi, the rebel sepoys were arrested from various areas of the valley and were tried by the British authorities of Cachar. In the report dated 13th February, 1858, Capt. Stewart said that he had engaged the Scouts in scouring the jungles in this vicinity assisted by mounted sepoys which succeeded in accounting for the 6 rebel sepoys, making a total of 185 killed since their entry in Cachar. Jyotirmoy Sen gives detail of the brutality of the Company's authority in dealing with the defeated rebel sepoys. Sen narrates that in order to create horror and terror in the heart of the common man, the rebel sepoys were executed after the trial by the Civil authorities of Cachar. They were hanged on the branches of the big *pipal* tree that stood on the north-west corner of the present Sadar Police Station of Silchar. A huge congregation of villagers was gathered around the spot by the beat of drums to witness the consequences of the revolt against the British Raj. In the same manner, two rebel sepoys were hanged on the branches of a *pipal* tree at a place on the bank of the river Dhaleswari at Company Ganj.

The Manipuri royal chronicle *Cheitharol Kumbaba* mentioned that King Chandrakirti sent a troop of 600 soldiers under Narneirakpam Menjor to Jiri along with Chingakhamba Pukhramba, Chingakhamba Dewan, Nepra Selungba, Sougaijamba Selungba, Nandababu Lairikyengba Hanjaba, Gokul Thakur and Ibungsija Haojoumacha Menjor. Manipuri scholar Pandit Kulachandra Sharma viewed that the team was led by Longjamba Roma Menjor. In a serious battle in the jungles of Jiri, Prince Narendrajit was captured by Major Roma on 20th January, 1858. After that, he was taken to Imphal on the 25th of January. But Capt. Stewart was in doubt about the attitude of the Manipur king towards the rebel Prince because he was actually the first cousin of the king himself. Therefore, he demanded that the rebel prince should be handed over to the British authority. Accordingly, as desired by the Political Agent of Manipur, M. McCulloch, King Chandrakirti handed over the rebel prince Narendrajit to the British authority of Manipur in the month of April 1858. It is said that King Chandrakirti definitely had some sympathy for the rebel prince Narendrajit Singh. So, he requested the Political Agent not to give him capital punishment. Since Narendrajit Singh belonged to Cachar, the British authorities wanted his trial to be conducted at Silchar. Accordingly, he was sent to Cachar in May 1858 and he was tried under the Act XIV of 1857. In the trial court, he was found guilty of waging war against the British Raj in India and subsequently, the Court recommended life imprisonment and he was deported to *Kalapani* (Andaman).

The revolt of 1857 was perhaps much more than a mere product of sepoy discontent. It was in reality a product of accumulated grievances of the people against the Company's administration and of their dislike for foreign rule. It began with a revot of the sepoy but soon engulfed wide regions and people. In the case of Manipuri Prince Narendrajit Singh, it is difficult to ascertain whether he had any ambitious plan to organize anti-British propaganda in the region. His father King Chourjit Singh lost the throne of Manipur due to the Burmese aggression in 1819. Subsequently, after the end of the First Anglo-Burmese War, as per provisions of the Treaty of Yandaboo, 1826. Gambhir Singha was recognized as an independent ruler of Manipur. Therefore, the deposed king Chourjit had to compromise with his long-cherished dream to regain his throne. But his son Narendrjit Singha never gave up the dream to regain Manipur. Meanwhile, in 1851 Chandrakiri Singha (son of Gambhir Singha) succeeded to the throne and was protected by the British according to the terms of the Treaty of Yandabo. 1826. Thus, the revolt of the sepoys of the 34th Native Infantry at Chittagong and their march towards the Barak plains gave them an opportunity to Narendrajit Singh to achieve his long-cherished goal, but he failed and this exposed him to British wrath.

However, the happenings in Barak Valley during the Revolt of 1857 could have turned otherwise. It could have spoiled the intentions of the Company authority in North East India. In this regard Capt. Stewart writes:

> "It must not be forgotten neither that Munnipuries (sic Manipuris) were once the rulers of Cachar and at no longer distance of time than the year preceding the invasion of this district by the Burmese. That this is borne in mind by them was fully revealed to me in the events which have recently taken place. When the mutineers of the 34th N.I. entered Cachar and their strength and intentions were unknown, the agitation

amongst the Munnipoorei population was extreme, and the station was threatened each day with the attack. Notice of this design came to me so often and from such different quarters that I could not but feel assured of their truth to a certain extent, and the account given by a scout, who was a prisoner in the camp of the mutineers when the Munnipoorie Prince Narendrajit Singh joined the enemy amply verifies my apprehension. This account was to the following effect that after recruiting themselves at Luckipoor the mutineers joined by the Munnipoorei population who were all prepared to assist, and possibly by the Hindustani sepoys among our troops, should return to the station, loot the Treasury and the Magazine, and make themselves master of the country after which an invasion on Munnipoor was contemplated and when Narendrajit Singh had fairly installed, he promised either to retain the mutineers in his own service or lead them through Assam and Nepal to their own Country."

In the context of the repercussion of the revolt of 1857 in Barak Valley, one may easily agree with the view that it was something more than a revolt but, something less than a National Revolt. However, it reveals that even though there might not have been any concept of independent India in the ideology of Prince Narendrajit Singh, his sense of space and outrage was to destroy anyone or anything that represented the alien British and to restore what he believed to have been his ancestral domain by taking advantage of the angst and hatred of the sepoys towards the British rule. This appears to be another very significant dimension of the Revolt of 1857 in its linkage with North East India.

7

Early Life of Narendrajit Singh (Ranjit Singh/ Sana Chahi Ahum) and the 1857 War of India's Independence

Koijam Swapan Singha

Narendrajit Singh (Ranjit Singh/Sana Chahi Ahum)

Manipur, also known as Kangleipak or Meitrabak, was once a small independent country in North East India. However, in 1891 A.D., the British occupied and gained complete control of the region after the Anglo-Manipuri War.

To picture the First War of India's Independence in Northeast India, one needs to understand the history of Manipur since Chourjit Singh's reign. Chourjit Singh became the king of Manipur in 1803 A.D. after Bhaigyachandra's son Madhu Chandra's reign and ruled until 1813. His brother Marjit Singh dethroned him, and the former fled to the Cachari kingdom. However, his reign was short-lived as he was dethroned by his brother Marjit Singh. Chourjit sought refuge in the Cachari kingdom, where he was granted an honourable residence.

Taking advantage of the Cachari King Gobindchandra's weakness, three Manipuri Princes, descendants of the dethroned Manipur king, began to rule Cachar in different parts. Chourjit established his kingdom in Dungripar in Sonai, controlling thirty-four villages. In Gumraha, Gambhir Singh ruled the western part of Cachar. At the same time, in the South, Marjit Singh established his kingdom in Jaffirbond, with the capital known as Konung Leikai, which means "capital village" in the Manipuri language.

Chourjit Singh had a big family with sixteen queens, eleven sons and six daughters. Notably, his fourteenth queen, Leirikyengbam Chanu Apanbi (Sakhi), gave birth to Narendrajit Singh or Ranjit Singh or Sana Chahi Ahum on April 27, 1819 A.D., in Dungripar near Sonai police station. Narendrajit was known as Sana Chahi Ahum for having spent three unusual years in his mother's womb. When Narendrajit was only seven years old, his mother relocated to Jaffirbond, the former capital of Marjit Singh. This move brought her closer to her sisters-in-law, Rajkumar Tribhubanjit, Rajkumar Ram Singh, and other Manipuri relatives who were guests of the British authority.

In 1832 A.D., Cachar was annexed by the British, leading to Chourjit's exile to Nadia with a meagre monthly allowance. The same year, 14-year-old Narendrajit Singh was trained in various war tactics to defend his homeland against British rule. According to Sagolshem Kula Singh, Kulaguru of Narendrajit, the training took place in locations like Kalapahar hillock in Lala Police Station, Hailakandi District, and sites like Thangjam Ching (Thangjam Hill) and Liklaipat (lake), where naval tactics were taught. Laishram Khagendrajit Singh said Narendrajit also established a training camp for 60-70 youths near Mglam village in Kalacherra police station. Remnants like Korfoo, Uyan, Pukham, Krishna Kanti Tengat and Chaishen are found in that place and are believed to be used by Narendrajit.

After the death of his brother Roma Singh in 1852, Narendrajit assumed the role of Leibakmapu, the nominal head of social administration in Jaribond Leibak. This tradition persists among Manipuris in the Hailakandi district, with Raj Kumar Meghajit currently holding the position. From 1852 to 1857, Narendrajit frequently visited the Tripura kingdom, where his brothers and relatives sought refuge. He secretly organized training for Manipuri youths and war preparations.

Between 1840 and 1841, Narendrajit and his brothers—Tribhuvan Singh, Ram Singh, Parbitor Singh, and Nilmoni Singh—attempted to invade Manipur but faced defeat. Narendrajit continued war preparations in Jaffirbond, knowing a significant conflict was imminent. Descendants of Bhaigyachandra—Bhuban Singh, Kanhei Singh, Nawal Singh, Sangou Singh, Khero Singh, Maipak Singh, and Sana Yeima Singh—visited Narendrajit during this time.

British authorities became suspicious of Narendrajit's activities with reports from James Davidson, South Cachar Tea Company manager at Gaglacherra near Jaffirbond. Davidson reported the meetings to Superintendent of Cachar Captain Robert Stewart. The British government began preparations to arrest Narendrajit and his team. In early September 1857, Narendrajit and five princes and twenty-seven followers headed to Dholeshwar in Agartala, where his brothers resided.

Narendrajit learned that the British Indian sepoy rebels had revolted and fled towards Tripura, led by Havildar Rujabuli Khan. Seizing the opportunity, Narendrajit joined the rebel sepoy leaders Ayudha Singh and Havildar Rujabuli Khan. He also sent two Manipuri youths to Jaffirbond to prepare for a fight against the British authority.

The rebel sepoys sought help from the Tripuri king. However, the king refused to help the rebel sepoy leaders, forcing Narendrajit to lead them eastward towards the border of East Bengal, the western part of Cachar. On December 18, 1857, at Maligarh near Latoo, the rebel sepoys engaged in a fierce battle with British sepoys, losing 30 men, including six Manipuris. Unfortunately, these Manipuris' names were not recorded by British authorities. The six rebels were: (i) Sagolshem Chauba, (ii) Thangjam Phulo, (iii) Thangjam Kalamohan, (iv) Thingom Ingenjao, (v) Laishran Bamcha, and (vi) Keisham Kunja.

Many Manipuri youths from Jaffirbond also joined the First War of Indian Independence against the British. British soldiers pursued the rebel sepoys and eventually entered Chandpur in Sorojpur Porgona near Hailakandi. They crossed the Kathakal river at midnight and took refuge on a small hillock. They were attacked by the British, resulting in the capture of 12 rebel sepoys, including two Manipuris. Some of the rebel sepoys were executed.

Narendrajit managed to escape to Manipuri Jungitila, located east of the Rangawti town near Hailakandi. On December 25, 1857, the rebels crossed Jalinga, Chatlabeel, and reached the foothills of Bhuban Hill. After spending some time in the foothills, Narendrajit and his team reached Binakandi on the morning of January 10, 1858, where they sought assistance from the local Manipuri population. Two Manipuri princes and many youths joined the cause.

The Cachar district records, page #351, letter #264 of 1857, dated December 7, reported by R. Stewart, mentions that the Manipuris rejected an intervention of Manipur in Cachar, and many ambitious Manipuri Princes have their eyes on Manipur.

The war of Binakandi finds mention in a letter to the secretary to the government of Bengal Fort William in #364 #8 of 1858, dated Cachar January 13, 1858.

> Sir,
> I have much pleasure in continuation of the formal letter to report the information that the lieutenant governor of the Manipuri, joined by Manipuri Princes and his followers, came out of the jungle into the village a little to the west of Binakandi yesterday morning at 10:00.

Another report, number 90, 1858, dated January 14, Page #366, mentions that,

> "It is now said that three Manipuri Princes had joined the 34 N.I. Before the last action, but with only 20 to 40 followers, these Manipuri Princes encouraged them, hoping to get abundant supplies at Lakipur. They were

joined by large forces of Manipuris assembled near the place to invade Manipur."

The book "The Mutiny Period in Cachar" published by Tagore Society for Cultural Integration Silchar, edited by Sujit Chowdhury, Page #42 mentions that when the rebel sepoys of the 34th Native Infantry entered Cachar, their strengths and intentions were not known. The agitation among the Manipuri population stemmed when Narendrajit joined the rebels. Contrary to the erroneous reports, the Manipuri participants joined the war to drive out the British from Cachar and potentially establish their kingdom there.

After the Binakandi war, Narendrajit and his warriors fled eastward, reaching the merging point of the Jiri River and Barak within Manipur's jurisdiction. There, they were confronted by Manipur levy troops dispatched by Chandrakirti Singh, the king of Manipur. A few rebel sepoys were killed, and Narendrajit was captured by Major Roma Singh and taken to Manipur with honour.

After a judicial trial by the British in Manipur, Narendrajit was sent to Cachar for further trial on May 10, 1857. British authorities tried him under Act 14 of 1857 and sentenced him to life imprisonment in the Kalapani prison, Andaman Islands.

In the latter part of 1858, no Manipuri princes remained in Cachar or British jails. Only a letter containing a reference to Kannai Singh, Hawjaw Singh, along with eleven other Manipuri princes, was dispatched to Nadia in Bengal.

In conclusion, Narendrajit, also known as Sana Chahi Ahum or Ranjit Singh, along with other Manipuri princes and warriors, played a significant role in the First War of India's Independence in North-east India, especially in Tripura, Cachar and Manipur.

8

Prince Narendrajit Singh

The Unsung Hero of Manipur in the War of 1857

Anandita Singh

Today, the 2nd of *Baisakh* marks the 203rd Birth anniversary of Prince Narendrajit Singh of Manipur—the patriot who fought the British for more than 2 decades without respite. We pay tribute to one of the most remarkable heroes of the freedom struggle who fought for the nation in the war of 1857 and led armies against the British troops in the Cachar region of Assam.

War of 1857: Planning and Execution

Imperialist schools of thought believe that the war of 1857 was merely a series of isolated 'revolts' or 'mutinies' in which the kings and queens participated only for their kingdoms and territories. Excerpts from the correspondence of Capt. Robt. Stewart, the then Superintendent of Cachar, paints a very different picture by clearly mentioning the circulation of *Chapati* and Lotus flowers throughout the country[1], thus, acknowledging that the nationwide planning for the war reached as far as Cachar and Chittagong. At Haridwar *Kumbh* of 1855, culture, strategy, and weapons shook hands and vowed to expel the British from Indian soil. The confluence of *Kumbh* meticulously planned the first war of Indian Independence of 1857. The myth of isolated uprisings in the country that has been propagated through years and generations, crumbles when we put historical evidence under a holistic lens. Under the circumstance of a lack of collective identity, goal, and a strong concept of 'nation', it would not have been practically possible to mobilize people from Delhi to Chittagong towards one common goal.

The Indians recruited in the British Army who were awakened by the call for action knew that the moment they defy orders of the British, they would lose their jobs, their livelihoods, and eventually their lives. So diligent was their planning that the messages of war were conveyed via lotus flowers and *chapatis* to the farthest and remotest corners of the country and so strong was the urge for self-determination among the people that they agreed to risk everything based on just one message because there was an inextinguishable fire in their hearts—the fire called *Swa*—that fuelled their passion for *Swaraj*.

Role of Prince Narendrajit Singh in the fight for Independence

Narendrajit Singh, a Prince of the Manipuri royal family was patriotically active in his capacity in Cachar. He was born on 2nd *Baisakh*, 1741 *Saka* (1819) to Chourjit Singh, the ruling king of eastern Cachar. Prince Narendrajit was a vigilante and observed the British interference in his kingdom very closely. The bottled-up resentment of the unwanted and unwelcomed intrusion took physical form in 1834 when his elder brother, Prince Tirbhubanjit Singh, led a battle against the British and the subservient Manipuri Kings who were bowing to the whims of the foreigners, and was mercilessly killed during the same. Narendrajit Singh followed the footsteps of his brother and joined the movement until he was captured in 1841[2] and sent to Dhaka jail. He was kept under surveillance in Dhaka for 10 years and was later released in 1851. During this period, the prince got acquainted with the then-Indian politics along with the resources, capabilities, and strategies of the British.[3] All this injustice towards his people taught him that until and unless a united Indian power confronted the British, their rule in India would not end. Hence, after the war of 1857 was planned at *Kumbh*, and Narendrajit Singh received information of the same, he began his endeavour to strike a blow on the British empire. According to his plan, he helped 6 other Princes of Manipur in escaping the British jails on 10th January, 1858.[4] After being released from Dhaka jail, Narendrajit Singh lived in Cachar where he mobilized both the people of Manipur and Cachar. His influence was so great that when the British instructed the king of Manipur to dispatch 400 troops to fight alongside them in 1857, and the King also agreed under pressure, the common people and the soldiers of Manipur refused to join the British serving troops. Based on the guidance of Narendrajit Singh, they rejected the British offer saying that they believed in the brotherhood of Indians and recognized the power of patriotism and secondly, they felt that it was sinful to fight for the foreigners who had encroached upon their territory.

Landmark in North-East: Cachar

Historians have also conveniently left out the north-east of India while documenting the war of 1857. But like the rest of the country, the fire of *Swa* was ablaze among the people here. A major chapter in this history was that of Cachar where platoons of freedom fighters from different regions converged and collectively fought the British under the leadership of Narendrajit Singh. Today, Cachar is a district located in Southern Assam. In 1857, it was a region that was a part of the British-occupied domains of India and a very important administrative centre. The above-mentioned movement towards Cachar began from the Chattagram or Chittagong hills, currently situated in Bangladesh, south of the Indian state of Tripura, by the awakened members of the 34th native infantry, on 18th November, 1857. To date, there is no official documentation of the names or even the exact number of soldiers that took part in this war for Independence. Some historians believe the number was 300 while others argue that the number was nearly 400-450.

The 34th Native Infantry of Chittagong

As per records, the movement of the 34th Native Infantry[5] started on 18th November, 1857, at 9-10 pm when the guards posted at the collector's office began firing rounds and thereafter released prisoners from the Chittagong jail. These released prisoners too joined the independence movement. Simultaneously, the British armory was attacked by the Indians from where surplus arms and ammunition were procured. Thereafter, as planned, they attacked the treasury and collected Rs. 2,78,267[6] and resumed their march in two separate branches—one towards Tripura and another towards Cachar, via the Lushai hills. Lt. Ross in his report mentions that the 34th Native Infantry had used careful strategy and split their platoon into smaller segments and took the forest route to reach Cachar. The branch that had taken the Aizwal-Silchar route to reach Cachar, was helped by local Lushai chiefs, also known as Sailo, from the Lushai Hills[7] in present-day Mizoram. The British had assumed that Indian patriots could be bought off with money and thus Capt. Stewart had made a failed attempt of luring the local chiefs to his side by promising Rs. 50 for every Indian soldier fighting against the British that they killed or captured. To put this in perspective, at that time gold price was Rs. 2 per Tola—10 grams, so it was a hefty reward. This offer was accompanied by a stern warning that the freedom fighters must not be helped. Contrary to what Capt. Stewart expected, the Lushai chiefs and common people alike helped them in whatever capacity they could. The branch moving towards Tripura was led by Rajabali Khan and after having been intercepted at Tripura by the British, had to take shelter in the hilly areas of Comilla, presently a border town in the Chittagong division of Bangladesh. This was the period where these soldiers of Indian soil faced the most difficulties.[8] Their ration stocks had been destroyed during the skirmish at Tripura, and they had been isolated in the thick jungles leading to Cachar where they had to sustain themselves in adverse situations. However, they were helped by the local people despite the British warnings and after having been replenished, the troops moved upward from Comilla to Latu, currently a town in the Karimganj district of Assam sharing borders with Bangladesh. At Latu, their movement was intercepted by Captain Byng who confronted them along with 150 soldiers.[9] A battle was fought at Latu on 19th December, 1857 and it marked a major victory for the freedom fighters as they were able to kill Capt. Byng and crush his platoon. C.E. Buckland records that after this battle, the winning party motivated the troops of Capt. Byng to renounce the British service and join the movement.

Combined Attack

When the 34th Native Infantry heard of Narendrajit Singh and his leadership, they decided to join hands with him and unite their forces. Hence, after the battle of Latu on 19th December, 1857, they entered Cachar on 20th December and met Narendrajit Singh and his followers. They launched a combined attack on the British at Binnakandi, currently a town in the Cachar district of southern Assam.

As the freedom fighters had strategized well, they could engage with the British on several fronts. This collective launch of attack by the Indian fighters gave a tough time to the British at Cachar, Mohanpur, Binnakandi, Latu, Jalingah, Govindnagar, and parts of Manipur. The leader of the movement, Narendrajit Singh was injured during the battle of Binnakandi on 12th January, 1858 by the British troops of Sylhet Light Infantry led by Lt. Ross.[10] Narendrajit Singh was then carried into the jungles of Manipur from where the king of Manipur, Chandra Kirti Singh, managed to shift Narendrajit Singh to the royal palace despite British pressure, on 2nd February, 1858. The king was totally against surrendering his kin to the British. They engaged in a series of exchanges over the custody of Narendrajit Singh, but eventually, the British got the upper hand and Chandra Kirti Singh had to surrender him on 25th April, 1858. After a show of trial, the British decided to send the leader of 1857 to the Andaman Islands for life imprisonment on 25th June, 1858.

Conclusion

Prince Narendrajit Singh was an exceptional leader with a sharp sense of judgment, observation, and leadership. He was a patriot who could mobilize people, inspire them, and lead them on the rightful path of freedom. Despite being banished from his land and suffering 10 years of wrongful captivity in Dhaka jail from 1841 to 1851, he never lost sight of what his country needed. To prevent any further influence of Narendrajit Singh on the people, the British exiled him to Andaman Islands as he was able to keep the fight going on for a much longer period than the British had expected and the leaders of North of India could sustain. Narendrajit Singh is a name that disappeared from the British records after 1858 but his name today is engraved in our history as one of the greatest freedom fighters. His relics, including a royal cloth, garland, *Paduka* (Footwear), *Shankh* (Conch Shell) and a handwritten copy of the *Bhagwad Gita*, have been preserved and revered by his descendant, Shri Birendrajit Singh in Agartala, Tripura. These are displayed once every year on Narendrajit Singh's Birth Anniversary. The troops of the 34th Native Infantry that left Chittagong had no clue of Narendrajit Singh until 19th December, 1857 and yet they fought proudly under his leadership in Cachar and Binnakandi because they believed that this Prince of Manipur could lead them to victory... and he did. This is not a legend of some unsung heroes, but a history of a people whose names have been conveniently omitted from the process of documentation, and thereof from our historical memory. The warriors of the 34th Native Infantry, the Lushai chiefs, and every single individual who contributed to the freedom struggle are the sparks of *Swaraj* that light up our lives till today.

Notes

1. Correspondence of Capt. Robert Stewart (Superintendent of Cachar) with the secretary to the government of Bengal, Fort William.
2. J.B. Bhattacharjee, *Cachar under British Rule in North East India*, New Delhi, 1977.

3. Anamika Dey, Anecdotes of Malegarh and Rontilla of Barak Valley, Assam, Pertaining to the Sepoy Mutiny 1857.
4. Roy, Jyotirmoy, *History of Manipur*, Imphal, 1973.
5. The 34th Native Infantry was initially destined to reach Dhaka and join hands with the 73rd Native Infantry and Collectively March to Delhi. Due to some setbacks, however, they had to change course and move towards Cachar.
6. Stewart's report, 16 January, 1858, cited in Sujit Choudhury (ed.), *The Mutiny Period in Cachar*, Silchar, 1981, pp. 23-24.
7. Capt. Stewart to the Secretary to the Government of Bengal, Fort William dated 7th December, 1857.
8. Subir Kar, *1857 in North East*, Akansha Publishing House, New Delhi, 2008, p. 80.
9. J.B. Bhattacharjee, *Mutiny in Cachar: A Survey of the Local Sources.*
10. Letter from Officiating Secretary, Foreign Department, Government of India, Fort William to the Secretary, Government of Bengal, No. 2272, 25 June, 1858, Mizoram State Archives.

Annexure 1

The Mutiny Period in Cachar*

Correspondence of Capt. Robt. Stewart, Supdt., Cachar, 1857-58

In order to show how far the Indian Mutiny of 1857 affected Cachar it might be worthwhile to trace a little of the history of the Mutiny itself. On January 23rd, 1857, the troops at Dumdum, near Calcutta, openly displayed their aversion to the cartridges supplied, and before that time there was general unrest indicated by the fact that *Chuppattis* began to circulate from village to village and there was also a similar circulation of lotus flowers, but these were among regiments only. No one knew where this began, but it was suggested that it came from Delhi.

On march 29th, the adjutant of the 34th Native Infantry was cut down on the parade ground at Barrackpore. This was followed by numerous incendiary fires at Barrackpore and in March and April twenty-five similar fires occurred at Umballa. At Meerut, the man of the 3rd Cavalry refused the cartridges, and on May 3rd, the 7th Oudh Infantry mutinied at Lucknow. The following Sunday while service was being held in the evening, the Cavalry and two infantry regiments broke the jail, released their comrades, murdered every European on whom they could lay hands and hurried off to Delhi. The beginning of the Mutiny is usually counted from that day, May 10th.

---

*Sujit Choudhary (1960), The Mutiny Period in Cachar, Tagore Society for Cultural Integration, Silchar (Assam).

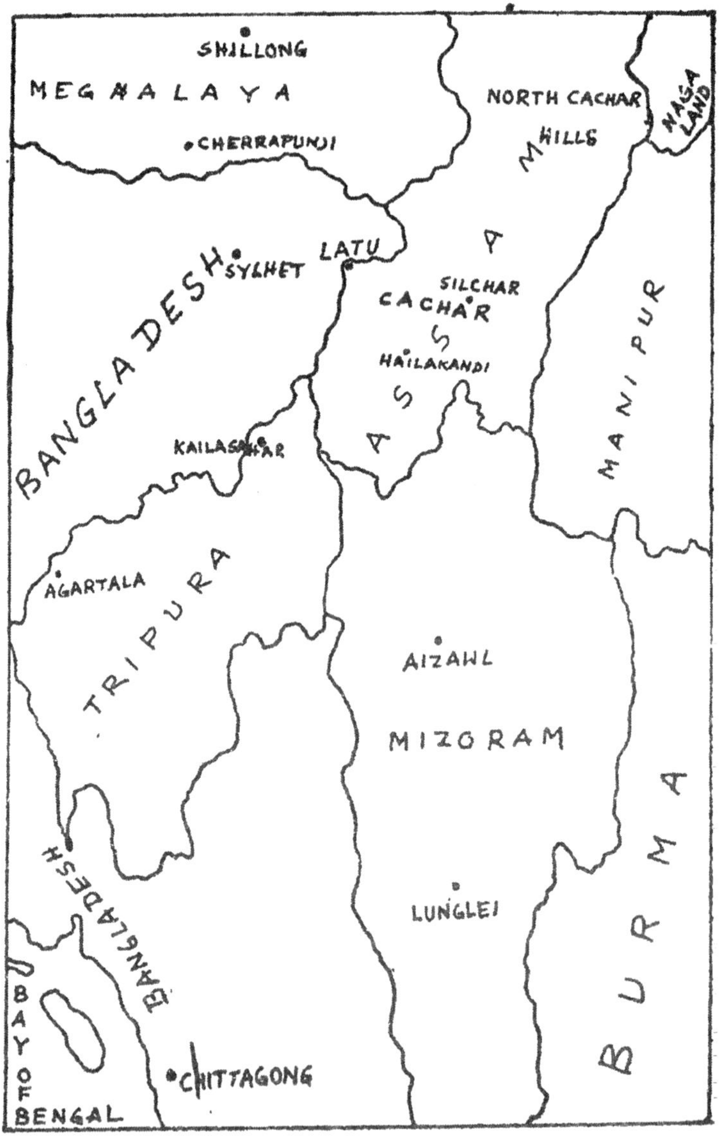
SHILLONG
MEGHALAYA
CHERRAPUNJI
NORTH CACHAR HILLS
NAGA LAND
ASSAM
BANGLADESH
SYLHET
LATU
SILCHAR
CACHAR
HAILAKANDI
MANIPUR
KAILASAHAR
AGARTALA
TRIPURA
AIZAWL
MIZORAM
BANGLADESH
LUNGLEI
BURMA
BAY OF BENGAL
CHITTAGONG

We can now see how it affected Cachar. It is obvious that the Superintendent of Cachar had been warned to send weekly reports and from June 10th until December the following reports were sent beginning with this letter.

"To the Secretary to the Government of Bengal,

Fort William,

From R. Stewart, offg. Supdt., Cachar

Dated, Cachar, 10th June, 1857.

Sir,

I have the honour to acknowledge the receipt of your letter No. 2509 of the 23rd ultimo, and I have much pleasure in reporting for the information of His Honour that the popular mind in Cachar seems in no way affected by the disturbances which are occurring in the North West. The Bengalee proclamation received by me was duly distributed, and the condition of the district is as peaceable as it possibly could be, there being no appearance of popular movement or excitement deserving of any notice. Regular reports will be transmitted on Saturdays."

From the 13th of June and until December, the following letter is sent each week:

"I have the honour to report for the information of the Lieutenant-Governor and in continuance of my letter dated 10th inst. that all remains quiet in Cachar."

But on the 7th December, 1857, the following letter is sent to the Secretary to the Government of Bengal:

"Sir

1. I have the honour to report for the information of the Leut. Governor of Bengal that having received intelligence of the Mutiny of the 3 companies of Sepoys at Chittagong, and of their having quitted the high road in the march north west, and entered the hill to the east, and being also put on my guard as to the chance of their continuing their march eastwards among these hills, and perhaps debouching into

the plains at Cachar I have also taken the following measures to have them opposed.

2. His Honour knows that the country directly south of Cachar is a vast tract of hills and jungle occupied by an independent and savage tribe called the Lhoochai, who at one time used to give us considerable trouble, but with whom our relations have been most amicable for some years past.
3. If the mutineers continue their march eastward they must pass through the residences of these people, and such is the intricate nature of the country, that if opposed by the inhabitants they would have but little chance of escaping, but would, in my opinion, be almost sure to be cut off in sudden attacks and ambushes.
4. I have therefore sent a small party bearing a token from me to the villages of Lhoochais, with messages to the following effect. That if men come to them through the jungle from the west with red coats and heavily laden, they are our enemies and must be opposed in every possible way, if it is the wish of the Lhoochais to endeavour to please our Government. That the men themselves are most probably wealthy, and it will afford easy and good plunder, and that moreover I will give Rs. 50 for each sepoy for whom they account to me.
5. I have guards posted at the two chief approaches from the south, and have scouts occupied in the same direction to bring me intelligence should the mutineers make their appearance by if they are coming this way at all, I am of the opinion that the march they have undertaken is more hazardous than they expected, and that such a small body offering such a rich prize to the savage and warlike people through whom they travel will have no chance of escape.
6. Should however they make good their march and enter Cachar, small as is the number of sepoys we have got in the place, and although the guns were the other day withdrawn to Sylhet, I hope we will be able to give them a warm reception.

7. I trust the arrangement I have made with reference to the advance of these mutineers will give satisfaction to His Honour the Lieutenant-Governor of Bengal.
8. The party I have deputed to the Lhoochais country not being part of my establishment I shall submit hereafter a bill for expenses incurred by their deputation for the sanction of the Lt. Governor.
9. In conclusion I would strongly urge upon His Honour the expediency of posting more troops in this district. Most of them at present in Cachar are detached in small outposts, and but very few remain in the Sudder station. Hardly a soldier can be withdrawn without difficulty, should any emergency call for the services of a small body in the field, and should a party of Munipoories now start on an invasion on Munipoor, as has been so frequently the case before, I should have no men to send after them to assist the Rajah as it is required of me to do. Moreover, the withdrawal of the guns and the sepoys accompanying them have given rise to reports, in which although there is little dependence to be placed, yet must have originated in something. Rumour says that an invasion of Munipoor has been projected among the Munipoorie of Cachar, and that it is intended that an attack should in the first place be made on the Magazine here for the purpose of obtaining a supply of ammunition for the expedition.
10. I neither credit the above in its entirety nor do I think that were the attack made it would meet with anything but complete failure. But still with so many ambitious Munipoorie Princes in the country who have their eye upon Munipoor and who cannot have failed to perceive the removal of our guns and sepoys from this place and to fancy that we were much weakened thereby and could not oppose their object, I think some movement on their part imminent, and trust that His Honour will agree with me, and put into my possession the means of averting it".

The following Saturday Stewart again reports that all remains quiet and the same report is sent in on the 19th of December. But on December 22nd, Stewart writes to the Secretary to the Government of Bengal.

1. "...............late on the night of the 19th instant I received a letter from Mr. Dodd, who had accompanied the force sent with Major Byng from Sylhet in pursuit of the mutineers of the 34th N. Infry; informing me that after having marched to Pertabghur Major Byng's force, upon certain information received countermarched to Latoo on the river Khosiara, and there had an engagement with the mutineers on the morning of the 18th, in which they were completely routed with a loss of about 30 men. The remainder had fled, it was said, in the direction of Pertabghur with a view to make towards Cachar and Munipoor.
2. Upon receipt of this information I immediately directed Lt. Ross, Comdg; the Detachment S.L. Infry; at this station to proceed with 50 men of his Regt; to which I added 25 of the Kookie Levy, and take up position at Panchgan, a village twelve miles to the west of this, which commands the western entrance into this district along the river, and is also a favourable position with reference to any operations along the line of hills running south, forming the boundary between this Zillah and Sylhet, and where it is now probable that the mutineers will endeavour to cross.
3. Lt. Ross started early on the morning of the 20th and has directions to remain at Panchgan until he hears certain intelligence of the movements of the enemy, when he is desired to act upon his own discretion. But upon being foiled or in the event of the mutineers escaping anywhere to the east of him, he is to fall back again on the Sudder station.
4. I have directed the Darogahs of my two thannas in that direction to report immediately to Lt. Ross any information they may receive and have also ordered the scouts, I have

detached to the south and west, to make their reports to the saine officer.

5. Since Lt. Ross' departure I have received a letter from the Darrogah of Latoo in Sylhet, informing me that the mutineers had passed the night of the 19th at Devalia Bunn, in Sylhet. I have also received a letter from chowdhury of Juffirghur in Sylhet, apprising me of their having gone Eastward with a view to cross over the hills into my pergunnah of Serespore and Hyliakandy, both these letters I communicated on that day I received them (21st) to Lt. Ross.
6. I heard yesterday from Lt. Ross, who still remained at Panchgan. He forwarded to me a note from Lt. Sherer, who on Major Byng's demise has assumed command of the Detachment on the field in Sylhet. He mentions that the mutineers have split into 3 or 4 different parties and all made for the east; one party 40 to 50 strong, he reports as having gone in the direction of Budderpoor which is close to Lt. Ross' position. But I am inclined to believe the reports which point to a more southern portion of the Serespore range as the place of their crossing.
7. Consequently on Lt. Ross' detachment with 75 men, the Sudder station being weakened in troops, I have drawn in several guards from the north and east, to reinforce it, and have now nearly a hundred sepoys under arms at this place. An outpost at Jalinga to the south-west I have relieved by placing in the stockade 12 armed Kookies from a village in the grant of the Cachar Tea Company, having withdrawn the men of the levy who were posted there. To the Kookie villagers, while so employed, I have promised the pay of sepoys.
8. I have also entertained a temporary establishment of 10 men as scouts, for the procurement of intelligence and collection of supplies, and have increased the police establishment of the 3 Thannas of my district by 8 Burkundazea, four for the

Sudder Thanna and two for each of the others for the same purpose.

9. I hope that the arrangements I have made will meet with the approval of His Honour. They would have all been made before had there been any sure intelligence of the intentions of the mutineers. But the latter having all along confined themselves to the Southern Jungles of sylhet, I was not assured of their near approach until Major Byng met them at Latoo and until then had only employed the fixed establishment at my disposal, and then too only to the south of my own district towards which, according to all reports, the mutineers were making.

P. S.: I have just received a note from Lt. Ross stating that having heard of the mutineers being on the western slopes of the Serespoor Hills, near a village called Companygunge, he marched last evening with a view to intercept them. The only fear now is that they may march too during the night and crossed the valley and escaped him."

On the 24th December, Stewart again writes:

"1. Lieut. Ross having heard of the mutineers as being at Chandpur in the Pergunnah Serespore, marched up the Hyliakandy Valley, starting on the evening of the 21st from Panchgoan. He reached Companygunge early in the morning of the 22nd but found that the mutineers had crossed the valley during the night and made for the hills and Jungles on the Eastern side opposite the Mouza of Mohunpoor.

2. Crossing the valley during the day, he entered the hills and encountered the enemy who had taken up their position on a hillock within the heavy Jungles. The ground appears to have been in every way unsuited for fighting, the jungle being thick, but an engagement took place in which some dozen of the mutineers were killed, the remainder escaping through the jungle to the south-east. The loss on our side was one man killed, three wounded and one missing.

3. Night having come on and my direction to Lt. Ross being to fall back upon the station should the mutineers escape him to the east, in order that fresh measures might be organised in another direction, he returned here yesterday morning.
4. Reliving the men he brought with him, I immediately despatched Lt. Ross with 75 men, to the Chutla Bheel, where it is expected the mutineers will next make their appearance. He will have there as auxiliaries some 40 armed Kookies belonging to the Cachar Tea Company, to whom I supplied muskets ammunition a few days ago.
5. With regard to the station itself I have placed pickets all round the threatened directions to give notice of any approach and we are quite prepared to meet them if they come. But they are much weakened by hunger and fatigue, and will not, I think, face the open country.
6. The conduct of the S.L. Infry is said to have been most excellent throughout the engagement which took place. Distant not more than 30 yards from the enemy while firing, the latter tried to gain them over by every art of appealing to their religious feelings as well as nationality. Failing this they taunted them by calling them "KRISTIAN KA KOOTAS" and "GOLAMIES" but they received for answer only bullets and abuse.
7. I have not had a single letter, note or communication from Sylhet for the last four days, and do not know anything of what is going on in that direction or what measures are being undertaken to reinforce me here. The mutineers are still two hundred strong and I have not anything like equal numbers to oppose them. Superior numbers are required in order to surround them in the jungle, else it will be nothing but a running fight the whole way through to Munipoor, whither it is now certain that the 34th are bent upon going. I am not even strong enough to despatch a force after them should they get out of my district and pursuing force would be most desirable.

8. I have kept Captain McCulloch well informed of the events which have been taking place and have desired him to put the Rajah on his guard.
9. Two of the 34th have been brought in as prisoners and are being tried by me today."

On the 26th of December the following letter appears :-

1. "........Lt. Ross again came upon the mutineers on the afternoon on the 24th instant in the valley of the Jalinga whither I had sent him on his return from Hyliakandy.
2. The mutinners showed no fight but fled after the first Volley, our men in pursuit firing into their tear and killing several. In their flight the enemy have thrown down several muskets, their bags of rice and of rupees, and ran to make for the south-east escaping into the dense jungle in that direction.
3. Lt. Ross returned to the station yesterday, which was a bad move as it has lost us one day, and has added twelve miles to the march of our troops. But not being able to follow them up directly, he returned, without doing so in a parallel direction, which he might have done had he been better acquainted with the country.
4. I have now send him to Kazeedhur in Bundraj, still further to the east. There again to await the exodus of the mutineers into the plains and I hope my plan will prove successful.
5. A detachment of the Sylhet Light Infy., under Captain Stevens will be here to-day. These I intend despatching to Singerbund, south of Luckipoor, where they will have a good chance of intercepting the 34th should they escape Lt. Ross and whence should they enter Munipoor. Captain Stevens will follow with a view of assisting the Political Agent and the Rajah.
6. The people of this district are much alarmed, the Bengalees being in the greatest of fear. The budmashes are all on the look out for a favourable opportunity to plunder and one considerable dacoity has already taken place.

7. The Munnipoories in Cachar seems anxious to take hold of this opportunity to carry out their views with reference to their own country and are intriguing and plotting an invasion of Munnipoor. I have three of their Princes under arrest on suspicion.
8. The two prisoners taken by the detachment, Sylhet Light Infantry, were tried by me and shot on the 24th instant. The usual form herewith enclose.
9. The report in Sylhet of the entire dispersion of the mutineers after the action at Latoo is wrong. They are still 200 strong with abundance of arms and ammunition and have determined purpose of pushing eastwards under the mistaken impression that they can go via Munnipoor to Nepal and hence to their own country."

Cachar, 26th December, 1857.

To

Captain Stevens,
Comdg. Sylhet Light Infantry.

Sir,

1. I have the honour to bring to your favourable notice the conduct of the marginally noted men of your Battalion.
2. These men formed a guard sent with 4 boxes of ammunition to Major Byng at Pertabghur. Thither they went but on reaching that place they found Major Byng had proceeded to Latoo.
3. They followed him down the valley of Pertabghur to Latoo and after the action were again sent off to Cachar by Lt. Sherer. On their way they encountered some fugitive mutineers and made prisoners of two of them whom they brought into me.

I have, etc.
R.S. STEWART,
Offg. Supdt.

The names of eight men are in the margin, SROOP SING, RAMDEEN SING, PARIAK SING, DAMEER SING, RAJCOOMER SING, SORRA RAM, KUJUNDER SING AND LUCHMEN SING.

The next letter is dated 2nd January, 1858:

1. "............ After the fight at Jalingah the mutineers pursued a south-eastern course and entered the heavy and dense jungles of Chuttla Howar, where they remained wandering about for five days, during this time they did not obtain one particle of nutritious food, but were compelled to eat jungle roots and berries.
2. They were tracked up by Kookie scouts and were found not to be making more than four miles a day and that too in a circuitous direction. The scouts came across several of them who had died of hunger and disease and also on the bodies of several of their children whom they had dashed on the ground being unable to carry on. The scouts also killed two sepoys, stragglers and made prisoners of a Chittagong Kaider and a Seikh Faqueer.
3. These scouts were the men of Kookie village on the lands of the Cachar Tea Company, supplied by me with fire-arms, and I beg to bring to your Honour's favourable notice the conduct of Mr. James Davidson, the manager of that company, who directed them and who during the five days that the mutineers were wandering in the wilderness, kept me continually supplied with excellent and reliable information concerning their movements.
4. His Honour will perceive that during the time that they were thus wandering in the jungles, natural causes alone were acting against them as not to call for direct opposition on the small force at my disposal. But when I heard of their having approached the eastern parts of the jungles facing the Pergunnah of Bunderaj, I directed Captain Stevens, who was posted by me with one hundred men at Sinaimookh,

to proceed with 50 picked men to their rear and drive them down upon Lt. Ross, who taken up a position at Nugdingram in the Bunderaj, when they would have been placed between two forces.

5. Before however Captain Stevens received my communication he had at the requisition of Lt. Ross moved down with whole force to Negdingram. The circumstances of this move were as follows:—

   The mutineers had come across the Kheddar establishment of Major Smith in the heart of Jungles and had driven them in on the night of the 30th, plundering them of about a day's provisions. I am not able to and out if this Major Smith later turned to tea, Mr. A. M. Smith at one time inherited Dholai and Kukicherra. The exaggerated reports given by these people of the numbers and desperation of the enemy had impressed Lt. Ross with the idea that his 75 men might not be able to cope with them, and he accordingly sent for assistance.

6. On the morning of the 31st, the mutineers debouched into the jungles of Bundraj, and were immediately attached by captain Stevens and Lt. Ross. They did not wait the assault, but immediately took to flight and crossing the Soonai River entered the jungles on the east side. The firing of our men was at too great a distance to make much affect but I learned from prisoners since taken that both the Subadars of the party were severely wounded.

7. Captain Stevens' march from Soonaimook rather disconcerted the plans I had arranged. He had been posted there with a view of marching to Binnakandy, where the rebels had crossed the Soonai and of intercepting them there while Lt. Ross followed up in the rear. When I requested him to move with 50 picked men to the rear of the enemy while west of Soonai, the 50 he would have left behind at Soonaimukh, reinforced by Lt. Binst. who had arrived with 50 more on the 31st, were ready to have taken the same place. Now, however,

Lt. Ross. and Captain Stevens with 175 men being together in the rear of the enemy, Lt. Binst with 50 has been placed by me at Captain Stevens disposal to be employed as he may direct.

8. The march of the mutineers will now lie through the dense jungles at the foot of the Booban-range, which they will skirt. My instruction to Captain Stevens are to follow them alone the plains in a parallel direction, keeping a little to their rear and preventing them from coming out to forage within the cultivated lands, also to send in his Lieuts, with strong parties to take up positions with the jungles to their front, thus bringing them between fires. With these instructions Captain Stevens has advanced to Gobindnagar and Lieut. Ross has been sent on to Casstainpoor.
9. I will not fail to communicate for the information of the Lt. Governor any subsequent operation which may take place and I hope that what has already been done will meet with his approval. The mutineers have not been able while in Cachar to inflict the slightest injury on the Government or the people. Confined to the densest they (the mutineers) have been brought to lowest physical condition of human beings, the prisoners taken being reduced to living skeletons. They have been met and beaten at each of the three places where they endeavoured to enter the plains, and are broken in spirits and reduced in number, although Captain Stevens still reports them at 150.
10. A jemadar and 16 men of the Sylhet Light Infantry dispatched from Sylhet after 10 of the mutineers who had separated from the main body at Latoo, pursued them into my district, overtook them at Mohimpoor in Hyliacandy, killed 8 of them and the remaining two were captured by my police.
11. Four sepoys, a bheestee, 3 women and children were brought in prisoners to-day by Major Smith's Kheddah Establishment and besides these there are now in my jail 5 more belonging

to the party all awaiting trial. Captain Stevens is also cutting off foraging parties and stragglers on his march.

12. From Munnipoor I have heard from Major McCulloch that the Rajah has despatched 400 men towards his frontier to give assistance and to cut off the mutineers should they cross the border. His force has been placed under my orders and I have directed the Major Commanding to confine his operations solely in the Munnipoor territory. He has my orders to halt at Noonshinbong, and to send to Luckipoor for provisions, where I have made arrangements to supply him, and also 100 men of the Sylhet Light Infantry, should it be necessary to send them into Munnipoor after the rebels.

Cachar, 9th January, 1858.

1. "........... The mutineers of the 34th N.I. are still in the jungle at the foot of the Boobun range of the hills, hemmed in by parties of the Sylhet Light Infantry on all sides.
2. Since last writing to you the mutineers have only on one occasion been able to procure rice, and this they did by a sortie of 50 men upon the village of Govindnugger on the skirts of the jungle while our troops were absent in another direction. One or two houses were there plundered and about a day's supply for their band secured.
3. To prevent similar forages on their part all the small villages skirting the jungles have been emptied and scouts have been posted in all directions to give instant notice of their approach.
4. The mutineers are supposed to have with them three or four Bengalees as prisoners and for the purpose of showing them the way, and it still seems to be their intention to make for Munnipoor.
5. Captain Stevens penetrated into the jungles on the 7th instant as far as Doorum Bheel, with a view of coming across the enemy, but he saw no trace of them, so extensive and dense are the wastes in which they lie at present concealed.

6. I have directed the Major Commanding the Munnipoor Force to detach 100 men to the confluence of the Jheeri and the Barak, there to await on their own side of the frontier the coming of the rebels. If able to get as far, it is likely that this will be the point of their passage. But little dependence however is to be placed on the Munnipoor Troops and I doubt much whether there are 20 men among them who have ever fired a gun."

13th January, 1858.

1. "...... The Mutineers, joined by a Munnipoor Prince and his followers, came out of the jungles into a village to the west of Binnacandy yesterday morning at 10 O'clock.
2. Lt. Ross was at that time stationed at Binnacandy with 100 men and Captain Stevens at Luckipoor with remainder of the force mounting to 150. Of the latter he had just despatched 50 under Lt. Binst, at my request, to strengthen the Sudder Station.
3. This party while proceeding along the northern bank of the river, a short distance from Luckipoor, was fired upon by the mutineers from the opposite bank. This fire was returned by Lt. Binst and the enemy engaged in front.
4. Lt. Ross then advanced from Binnacandy along the southern bank of the river, and attacked their right flank. Captain Stevens and Lt. Binst crossing the river in rafts under cover of this attack, and an action took place which lasted for two hours. The mutineers were beaten from house to house in the village they occupied and at last dispersed and fled back into the jungles to the south, pursued by our troops as long as it was practicable.
5. Seventeen dead were counted on the field among whom was a Jemadar. Two sepoys taken prisoners were shot, and one straggler of the retreating rebels killed by the scouts, making a total of 20 killed besides numbers who must have been badly wounded in the engagement. On our side we lost two men killed and two badly wounded.

6. The conduct of the men both of the Sylhet Light Infantry and the Kookie Levy is described by Captain Stevens as being most excellent, and I am sure his Honour will perceive that, to the European officers leading the force, the greatest credit is due for the promptness and precision with which they acted, and which secured a victory so decisive and effectual.
7. Doctor Shircore was present with the force in the double capacity of medical officer and in charge of the intelligence department. To his indefatigable exertions Captain Stevens is indebted for the good information which he has all along received of the position and design of the enemy.
8. The sudden withdrawal of the European troops from Sylhet has had no good effect in this district and some of the Munnipoories have been incited to take up arms in favour of the Princes with a view to accompanying the mutineers into Munnipoor and usurping the Government of that country, although they were very quiet before. The prince (supposed to be Norindrojeet Sing) has already joined them and six Princes whom I had placed under arrest here to keep them out of mischief have managed to make their escape and will doubtless do the same.
9. Great doubts are entertained of the fidelity of the Munnipoor army and it is supposed that they would have no objection to a chance of dynasty in their own country. But they have hitherto obeyed the orders I have transmitted to them, and their officers (likely to be favourites of the present Rajah) vouch for their loyalty.
10. The fight at Binnacandy will have the best effect and has not only dispersed the mutineers but will serve to cool the ambition of those princes, who have not as yet actually committed themselves, as well as tend to keep the Munnipoor force true to their allegiance.
11. In the event of an advance upon Munnipoor being effected by the enemy, I have given directions for a party of 100 men to proceed at once into the valley to afford assistance to Major McCulloch and the Rajah.

12. Three sepoys of the 34th N.I. taken prisoners by the villagers were tried, sentenced and executed by me the day before yesterday, and 2 stragglers of a party of eight that had separated from the main body after the action at Nogdirgram were killed yesterday by a small party sent out after them.
13. In conclusion I trust that his Honour will be pleased with what has been done and will mark with a sign of his approval the gallant and loyal conduct of the troops and the vigour and energy of the officers who led them."

13th January, 1858

To

Lieutt. T.G. Ross,
Combg. Detachment Sylhet. L.I.B.

"I have great pleasure in transmitting to you the accompanying copy of a letter received from the Government of Bengal, thanking you and the men under your command for the gallantry and loyalty displayed by you in action with the enemy at Mohunpoor in Hyliakandy.

I trust that it is not necessary for me to assure you how cordially I myself congratulate you upon the success which then and subsequently, has attended your exertions."

16th January, 1858

"1. I have the Honour to enclose weekly statement of mutineers tried and executed by me under Act XVII of 1857, during the past week.
2. Since the action at Binnacandy, the mutineers have not shown themselves, but are reported by the scouts to be still in the jungles to the south, at the foot of the Boobun Hills and broken into parties of 4 and 5.
3. It is now said that three Munnipoor Princes had joined the 34th N.I. before the last action, but with only some 20 or 30 followers, and that these Princes encouraged them with

hopes of getting abundance of supplies at Luckipoor, and of being joined by a large force of Munnipoories collecting near that place for the purpose of invading Munnipoor.

4. Of these, three Princes it is reported that two have since deserted the mutineers and that the third is still with them being kept as a prisoner.
5. I have desired Captain Stevens to make no distinction between the mutineers and the Munnipoories with them.
6. I have rewards for Rs. 100 for the apprehension or betrayal of each of the Princes who have effected their escape from us, and also for that of Nrindrojeet Sing, who is supposed to have joined the rebels.

   I have also directed the attachment of all the property, both land and moveables, appertaining to them in Cachar, and likewise that of their followers, and I trust these measures will be confirmed by His Honour, the Lieut. Governor.
7. Seven other Princes against whom rumour had began to be busy have been apprehended by me and placed under close arrest.
8. At my request a night march is to be made this evening on the village Lalong, in the neighbouring jungles of which it is reported that the Princes are collecting followers and I trust that it will result in the capture of some of them.
9. Since the affair at Binnacandy 3 mutineers, stragglers, have been caught and shot by Captain Stevens in Camp. This 63 bonafide sepoys of the 34th N.I. counted killed since they entered Cachar.
10. As it is now apparent that portion of our own subjects in this district are in rebellion against the Government, I have the Honour to solicit that you will suggest to the Lieut. Governor the expediency of investing me with powers under Act XI of 1837 for the trial of such as may be apprehended."

Date..........

1. "......... Captain Stevens moved out yesterday at noon and entered the jungles at the foot of the Boobun Range with 80 men.
2. The mutineers have been reported to have collected themselves into two bodies, each of between 30 and 40 strong, but unable to combine, owing to the denseness of the jungles. It was to the position of one of these two bodies that the scout led Captain Stevens.
3. After several hour's march through the most intricate country and thick jungles, Captain Stevens came upon the enemy and took them by surprise while cooking. They were posted on a teelah or small hillock, and after exchanging volleys, our men charged up the hill driving the enemy from it, and dispersing them in all directions. Ten mutineers were counted dead on the field and many besides must have been wounded. One regimental barber and two women were taken prisoners, and 20 muskets were taken together with all the clothes and utensils of the party, attacked, those who escaped having nothing but lungoites (loin-clothes) on them. On our side there was no loss, either in killed or wounded.
4. From the statements of the prisoners taken, it would appear that this party have no more muskets among them, and therefore they have become harmless, and will be caught and brought in by the villagers.
5. The position of the other party in the jungle is not accurately known, but they are well watched and have not a chance to escape.
6. The operation of the troops during this week have been confined to expeditions into the jungles, similar to the one above recounted, but unsuccessful owing to the denseness of the jungles. The scouts have however being very successful in shooting stragglers and bringing in prisoners and the Rajah of Munnipoor's force have also taken several who were brought into our camp and shot.

7. The following is a list showing to the total numbers of mutineers, bonafide sepoys, killed since they entered Cachar:

Tried and executed by Civil authority	13
Killed in action	37
Died of wounds	2
Killed by scouts	17
Found dead in jungles	2
Caught by villagers, scouts, troops both Govt. and Munnipoorie, and tried and executed by Military Law	39
Total	**110**

8. The following individuals belonging to the camp of the mutineers have been taken prisoners and await trial :

Regimental Bheestie	1*(This person sentenced to 14 yrs transportation)
Regimentral Barber	1
Seikh Faqueer (Camp Follower)	1
Chittagong Convicts	10
Women (two badly wounded)	12
Children	7
Total	**32**

One child has died since taken, and one was accidentally shot during the action at Binnakandy. I have the honour to solicit the Lieut. Governor's instruction with reference to the disposal of the women and children. The convicts I am prepared to try when vested with the necessary powers.

9. I have before informed you that the Munnipoories have deserted the mutineers. I have as yet been unable to take any of the princes who joined them or who broke their arrest, but I do not think it possible that they can long escape, as the rewards offered for their apprehension will excite the cupidity of the Bengalees to give information.

10. I am preparing a list of the Munnipoorie Princes resident in Cachar for submission to His Honour through Mr. Allen, with a view to arranging their future disposal. The presence of so many of them (upwards of 30) in this district, almost all having some sort of claim or title to the Guddee of Munnipoor, has already on many occasions, and is likely to be in future also, the cause of much disturbance, which nothing short of their deportation further west is likely to prevent.
11. No prisoners have been tried by me during the past week under Act XVII of 1857, those taken being sent to camp and executed there by sentence of Drum Head Court Martial."

27th January, 1858

1. ".............. my head scout reported to Captain Stevens yesterday that he discovered the position of a small body of mutineers in the jungles, and Captain Stevens thinking it only one of the fragments of the body he had scattered on the 22nd sent out a party of 30 men under command of Bhuggutbeer Jamadar of the Sylhet Light Infantry to cut it up.
2. The Jamadar, led by the scout, proceeded into the jungles and after some search came upon the mutineers, but found that the small party seen by the scout had been joined by the remaining one of the two large bodies into which the mutineers had formed after the action at Binnacandy, and mustered in all some 40 or 50 strong.
3. These superior numbers, occupying a strong position on the hillock covered with thick bamboo jungle, were attacked by the Jamadar and his party and completely routed. Thirteen were left dead on the field and the remainder including one who was very severely wounded managed to effect their escape.
4. The conduct of the Jamadar Bhuggutbeer and his men is worthy of great praise, the more especially as they came

unexpectedly upon such a large body, when they were looking about for a few stragglers only, and I trust that His Honour will mark it with his approval.

5. Independently of the 13 killed in this last affair, 14 have, since the date of my last letter, been killed, making a total of 137 killed since they entered Cachar. This together with number accounted for in Sylhet, viz. 44, makes 181, so that there cannot be many of them left afoot now.
6. The mutineer still remain in the same dense jungles, and are fairly caught in a trap out of which they possibly cannot escape."

30th January, 1858

"1. Since last letter I am happy to state for the information of His Honour the Lt. Governor of Bengal that the mutineers of the 34th N.I. have been caught and brought in by twos and threes, by my scouts and villagers, and that the number killed in Cachar now amounts to 162. This when added to the number supposed to have been killed in Sylhet would show a total of 206, besides which many must have died in the jungles of starvation and of wounds, of whom we do not know.

2. I have not been informed as to what was the actual strength of the mutineers when they left Chittagong, but I suspect that we have come pretty nearly to the end of them. I have therefore directed the Munnipoorie force that were sent by the Rajah, to fall back upon the valley, leaving only a few men to guard the passes and Lt. Ross still remains at Binnakandy with 140 men, as much to guard against the machinations of the Munnipoorie Princes as to account for any surviving mutineers."

2nd January, 1858

1. "........ Norindrojeet Sing, the chief of Munnipoorie Princes, who joined the mutineers before the action of Binnacandy

has been apprehended in Munnipoor by the Rajah and is now in confinement in that place. The Prince has a severe wound in the foot which he is supposed to have received at Binnacandy and cannot at present be removed from Munnipoor. I have written to the Political Agent to send him in at once should he happen to be taken in that direction, and I have now the honour to solicit His Honour's instructions as to his disposal when he arrives.

2. Norindrojeet is a first cousin of the present Rajah, and although seriously opposed him, being himself a claimant to the throne, still I anticipate that it will be with some reluctance that the Rajah will give him up to suffer the punishment which is his due.
3. The mutineers of the 34th N.I. may be said now no longer to exist. One hundred and sixty-nine sepoys and officers have been killed since they entered Cachar, and the remainder having thrown away their muske are trying to escape individually or in parties of 2 or 3.
4. Captain Stevens has returned to Cheerapoonjee, the H.Q. of the battalion, but Lt. Ross with 100 men of the Sylhet Light Infantry and 40 of the Kookee Levy is still after them."

To

MAJOR McCULLOCH,
Political agent,
Munnipoor,
2nd February, 1858

1. "............... It gives me much pleasure to hear of the capture of Norindrojeet Sing, and I trust that he will soon meet with the punishment he so well deserves.
2. A Kote Havildar and a sepoy of the 34th N.I. are supposed to have accompanied Norindrojeet when he left the mutineers force after Binncaandy. He having bound himself by oath to see them clear out of the company's territories. May I request the favour of your informing me whether anything has been

heard of them, and if not, of suggesting the expediency of questioning Norindrojeet on the subject.

3. It is just probable that Norindrojeet Sing may think it worth his while to deny having had any reasonable commerce with the mutineers at all, but the proof against him is completed both by means of our own scouts who were at time prisoners in the mutineers camp and through prisoners taken by us.
4. I think it would be most desirable were the Rajah to send small parties of men to be on the look out at the entrances to the valley on the west, such places as Rocbhooching and Simital, for then they might chance to get hold of any small parties of the mutineers who may have escaped our troops at Luckipoor, and have got on the road avoiding also the Munnipoorie force on the way. There may have been several who have been thus guided by the Bengalees and Munnipoories of Cachar for the sake of money."

On the fifth of February the following letter was sent to captain Stevens, Lt. Binst and Doctor Shircore:

"1. I have much pleasure in forwarding to you, together with my sincere congratulations, the thanks of the Government of Bengal to you and to the troops who served at Binnacandy.
2. The mutineers continue to be brought in by ones and twos, but they are now so completely dispersed that the troops have no chance of acting against them, and the operations are almost entirely confined to scouting.
3. The number accounted for in Cachar now amounts to 179, among the 17 killed since my last report were two subadars.
4. Having made over charge of the station to my assistant, Dr. Shircore, I came out here yesterday on circuit and to see how affairs were getting on. I fired the supposed position of the remnant of the mutineers to be in a belt of jungle close to this, and I have directed the whole to be fired, and propose to enter tomorrow with a line of elephants, mounting four

sepoys on each and breathing through. I daresay that this will be the means of driving the remainder out.

R. Stewart

Camp Luckipoor, 8th February, 1858

1. "............... The prisoner Nuttah Khan sentenced by me on the 9th ultimo to transportation for 14 years, although guilty of the offences charged against him being a Government servant, was not guilty, in my opinion, to the same extent as a regular sepoy, being simply a water carrier. Moreover his offence was somewhat exterminated by the fact of his having separated himself from the rest of the mutineers with the intention, as declared by him, of giving himself to me.
2. In like manner on the 26th ultimo I sentenced Jokoo, a barber, attached to the mutineers to transportation for life, he being also simply a camp follower, and not guilty to the same extent as the sepoys. The barber received however a severe punishment because he was actually taken in flight, and without any intention on his own part of yielding.
3. On the 4th inst. I sentenced a bunnia and the son of a sepoy to seven years' transportation only. They were both young men, of 17 or 18 years of age, and although arrived at years of discretion yet perhaps not quite responsible for their acts, being dependent on their seniors."

"To

Lt. Ross. Commanding in Cachar.

Dated Luckipoor, 13th Feb., 1858

1. There being no longer any necessity for the presence of so many troops in this part of the district, I have the honour to request that you will withdraw those under your command to the station, leaving only a party of 50 of the Sylhet L.I. under a native officer at Luckipoor.
2. The detachment left at Luckipoor will be posted at the godown guard house in this village and will purchase its

supplies and fire-wood from the neighbouring bazar, being furnished by the commt. at Silchar with those articles which are not procurable here."

13th February, 1858

1. "........... I have engaged in scouring the jungles in this vicinity with scouts and mounted sepoys and have only succeeded in accounting for the 6 mutineers, making a total of 185 killed since entering Cachar, in the following manner:

Tried and executed by the civil authority	14
Killed in action	57
Found dead in the jungles	8
Killed by scouts in the field	37
Brought in by troops, both Govt. and Munnipoorie Scouts, Kookies and villagers, and shot by sentence of Drum Head Court Martial	... 69
Total	**185**

The list of camp followers taken stands now as follows:

Regimental Bheestie	1	Transportation for 14 years
Regimental Barber	1	Transportation for life
Regimental Bunnia	1	Transportation for 7 years
Sepoy's son	1	Transportation for 7 years
Sheikh Faqueer	1	Awaiting Trial
Chittagong convicts	10	Awaiting Trial
Women	13	Awaiting Trial
Children	11	(two since dead)
Total	**39**	

3. It is possible that there may be one or two of these mutineers alive, but far more probable that they have died of starvation in the depth of the jungles; one or two may also have escaped back westwards but of those nothing certain is known, and I think the number killed must be very near indeed to that of the mutineers when they entered the district.

4. About 110 or 120 stands of arms have been taken from the enemy and about Rs. 30,000 of the plundered Chittagong treasure recovered, but of those I will send a detailed account when I return to the Sudder station, together with an account of the expenses I have been put to in giving rewards, etc.
5. The mutineers having been finished off and the rebellious Munnipoories being nowhere to be found, I do not think that it is necessary to keep much large detachments of troops any longer in the field. I have therefore directed Lt. Ross to return to the Sudder Station, leaving only 50 men at this place, and have ordered the withdrawal of the remaining portion of the Munnipoorie army to its own Headquarters."

15th February, 1858

1. "................ I forwarding a list of Munnipoorie Princes with a view to settling their future disposal............
2. .... I have the honour to request that you will be so good as to inform me who are the Princes most obnoxious to the Government of the Rajah of Munnipoor, and who in the opinion of that Government ought to be removed from Cachar............and how much the Rajah is prepared to pay towards their maintenance.
3. It is possible that the Rajah having got rid of many of the Princes out of his own country, and feeling assured of the protection of our Government, may demur to incurring any expense on their account. But it is necessary that he should be informed that his own house is on fire. It will not do to throw the burning brands on the thatch of another without contributing to the supply of water which is to put them out.
4. I think that the most equitable arrangement which could be entered into between the two Governments would be for the Rajah to name some four or five of those whom he principally suspects of entertaining sinister designs towards himself. The like number of the most troublesome in Cachar being afterwards nominated by me, and the expenses of the

maintenance of both at a distance from the Frontier equally shared.

5. The above is merely a suggestion and if not acceptable, I have no douht that many other arrangements will propose themselves, whereby the chronic state alarm, in which both Cachar and Munnipoor are uniformly placed by the ambitious designs of these Princes, may be removed."

To

Captain Dewaul, Comdg.

Detacht. Late 34th N.I.
17th February, 1858

1. With reference to the late mutiny at Chittagong and to the operations which have been undertaken against the mutineers of the 34th N.I. since they entered Cachar and Sylhet, I have the honour to inform you that 185 fighting then have been killed in this district and that 44 were killed in Sylhet and Tipprah, and request the favour of your letting me know how many of your men of all ranks left Chittagong, in order that I may determine the number at present still unaccounted for.
2. It is currently reported that one, Rajbullee Khan, a havildar, who is supposed to have been the leader of the rebels, has escaped westward, together with his wife, and one or two others. I have the honour to request therefore that you will furnish me with a description roll of this man, together with a description of his wife, if such also can be procured, in order that a hue and cry may be raised in the neighbouring district.
3. The Seikh Faqueer regarding whom you wrote to Captain Stevens was very fortunately saved by what you said of him from perhaps the severest punishment short of death, and I have no doubt that if you communicated with me more freely on matters connected with this mutiny, not only would

much more be elicited but the end of justice would be more equitably answered.

17th February. 1858

1 . ... I have the honour to forward the accompanying list showing the names and native places of the women captives taken from the mutineers of the 34th N.I.

2. I have also the honour to forward the accompanying extract from a private letter addressed to Captain Stevens by Captain Dewaull late in command of the detachment at Chittagong by which his Honour will perceive that the Seikh Faqeer, who was taken, may be held guiltless. This man was taken alone, and no money or valuables whatever were found upon him, which was not the case with the women, many of them being laden with rupees and ornaments. I request the favour of your being informed how the faqeer is to be disposed of.

The following letter, though only indirectly concerned with the Mutiny may be of interest, as it concerns the defence of Cachar, and incidentally of Tea Gardens.

20th February, 1858

1. .... I submit...........the following report upon the defences necessary for this District and to suggest the means of providing them with as little expense as possible to the state.
2. His Honour is aware that on three sides of Cachar we have an exposed frontier. On the North East lies the tract of country inhabited by the wild and savage tribes of the Angamie and Kutcha Nagas, who constantly attack and plunder the villages in the hills both of this district and of North Cachar, massacring all who may fall into their hands. On the south we have similarly wild and untameable tribes of Lhoochais and Pays, on whom no reliance is to be placed. And on the East the Independent State of Munnipoor.

3. For the defence of the North-eastern Frontier it is necessary to have guards posted in the villages upon line of boundary all along. And no less than four are thus situated at different villages in that direction. These guards have frequently and even lately been instrumental in protecting the villages at which they are stationed from direct attack, and such is their importance that if they were withdrawn the sites of the villages in the North East would immediately be deserted.
4. On the South also there are four guards stationed at stockade posts for the purpose of protecting our cultivation and the population in that direction from the ravages of the Lhoochais, and their presence is most beneficial, covering as it does all the Tea Plantations which have recently been taken up by Europeans in this district. Were these guards not pushed on towards the South, as cultivation extend in that direction, it would not be possible to get settlers to take up the fire tracts of waste lands which lie within our boundary on that side, much of which lands were in former times actually under cultivation, but obliged to be deserted owing to the pertinacity with which the Southern tribes continued their attacks. The Tea Planters would also find it difficult to induce the Bengalees to go over in that direction to labour for them, as the greatest fear prevails over the people, caused by the atrocities perpetuated by the Lhoochais in their warfare.
5. On the East, the State of Munnipoor, dependent on us for its integrity, and to which a European Officer is deputed as Political Agent, might seem to offer a safe and inoffensive Frontier, but in truth it serves only as a weak barrier or outpost between ourselves and the Burmese, a barrier which might at any time be easily surmounted by the latter power did it feel so inclined. The Munnipoorie army is I believe nominally 3000 strong but most inefficiently armed, all the muskets being old and most of them entirely unserviceable. It is much to be feared also that in case of an invasion of the Burmese, there would be a strong faction in Munnipoor in

favour of the invaders, as the Government of the present Rajah does not appear to be a very popular one owing to the fact of his being a descendant of a younger branch of the Royal Family, members of the older branches being in exile both in Burma and Cachar.

6. But it is not from fear of any direct attack either from Munnipoor or Burma that the presence of troops is necessary in Cachar with reference to our Eastern Frontier. Speedy intimation would doubtless bė given were any such movement contemplated by these two states, and troops could be concentrated from other points to meet it. It is from the fact that about one fourth of the population of Cachar itself consists of Munnipoories, most of whom have been banished from Munnipoor, or who have fled either from political causes or oppression. Among these are many members of the Royal Family, who lay claim to the throne itself, and where title is considerėd accordingly to the right of Primogeniture is superior to that of the present occupant. All, of these, both Princes and subjects, are actuated by but one wish, that of being able to return to their own country, This can only be effected by the ejection of the present Rajah, and the substitution of the Prince whose cause is at the moment most popular, and the consequence is that Cachar is made the theatre of intrigues carried on by these refugees against the Government of Munnipoor.

7. The services of Ghombeer Sing, the father of the present Rajah of Munnipoor, in the Burmese War of 1824-26 gained for him the throne of Muilnipoor after the Burmese had evacuated the country, and our Government continue to assure the succession to his descendants. It has always therefore been the duty of the superintendent of Cachar to frustrate any designs on the part of the Munnipoorie exiles in Cachar towards the Government of Munnipoor. But such is the clannish nature of this nation, so secretly do they conduct their plots and conspiracies speaking as they do a language

unintelligible to the rest of the inhabitants, and holding their meetings in the depths of the vast jungles of this district, that it has been found impossible to counteract them, until they have developed themselves and it can then only be done by the instrumentality of troops in the field.

8. It must not be forgotten either that Munnipoories were once the Rulers of Cachar, and at no longer distance of time than the year preceding the invasion of this district by the Burmese. That this is borne in mind by them was fully revealed to me in the events which have recently taken place. When the mutineers of the 34th N.I. entered Cachar and their strength and intentions were unknown, the agitation amongst the Munnipoorie population was extreme, and the station was threatened each day with attack. Notice of this design came to me so often and from such different quarters that I could not but feel assured of their truth to a certain extent, and the account given by a scout, who was a prisoner in the camp of the mutineers, when the Munnipoorie Prince, Norindrojeet Sing, joined the enemy, amply verifies my apprehension. This account was to the following effect. That after recruiting themselves at Luckipoor the mutineers joined by the Munnipoorie population who were all prepared to assist, and possibly by the Hindustanie sepoys among our own troops, should return to the station, loot the Treasury and the Magazine, and make themselves master of the country ; after which an invasion on Munnipoor was contemplated, and when Norindrojeet Sing had been fairly installed, he promised either to retain the mutineers in his own service or lead them through Assam and Nepaul to their own Country.

9. With such a spirit among the Munnipoorie population both towards the Government of their own country and towards our own, the necessity of keeping up a force in the district, sufficient at any time to quell any of their sudden insurrections, must be apparent, and in order to do this

it will be necessary, after providing for the defence of our southern and north-eastern Frontiers, and for the defence of the station itself, to keep about 150 to 200 men fit for immediate service in the field, ready in quarters.

10. The troops generally posted in Cachar consist nominally of 3 companies of the Sylhet Light Infantry, supposed to be 240 strong, but their numbers actually scarcely exceed half that strength ; and of the Kooky Levy numbering 200 bayonets. Of the Sylhet Light Infantry 25 form the escort of the Political Agent of Munnipoor and are to all intents and purposes ineffective for any purposed offensive or defensive in Cachar. Of the remainder 25 are posted at a stockade in Hyliakandy, and the rest exclusively occupied in furnishing guards for the defence of their own lines, the Treasury and the Magazine, leaving not a man available even for their own relief, much less for active service in the field should such be necessary. Of the Kookie Levy the general distribution is noted in the margin, and it will be seen that hardly a man of that body either, remains available for field service.

11. In addition to the guards which it has always been custom to post on our Southern and Northeastern Frontiers, and which are indispensably necessary, I feel it now requisite to keep a strong party posted at Luckipoor on the east, also to act as a check to Munnipoorie intrigue. Indeed ever since I obtained the superintendency of this district, I have had a small party of the Kookie Levy stationed there but it is a post requiring 50 men atleast. In addition to this and beyond the number of troops allotted for the defence of the Frontier, there ought to be, independently of troops for the relief of line and station guards, at least 120 men ready to move out of the station at a moments notice, without denuding it.

12. The Sylhet Light Infantry, appear to be too well occupied Westward to be able to afford to give the required numbers to Cachar. The small number already stationed here appear to be grudged, and on the occasion of slight emergency, such as

the dispatch of a Treasure party to Dacca, or anything of that kind, troops are generally drawn from Cachar. It is moreover probable that in default of other accustomed troops to the West, the services of the Sylhet Infantry, will be still further extended in that direction, and that fewer will be able to remain in Cachar.

13. Under the circumstance I would strongly urge upon the Government the expediency of increasing the numbers of the Kookie Levy for local service. It is a measure which I think, would be attended with less expense than any other, providing for the effectual defence of Cachar and the Frontier in general. In raising the Kookies we arm a people with neither Political power nor prestige but who are at the same time naturally brave and inured to this climate and to the warfare that the presence of so much jungle on this frontier is likely to offer. Further, we enlist a people in our service than whom no other could act as a better check against the Munnipoories. People who have no sympathy with the caste or creed of any other in Hindustan, and who are moreover bound to us, for the Protection they have received since they came into our territories.
14. Of the services of the few men of the Kookie Levy occupied in recent operations His Honour already knows. But the services of the Tribes do not end there, and about as many men of the mutineers of the 34th N.I. as were killed in action by our troops, were killed in separate conflict or brought in as prisoners by the Kookie villagers whom I had organised for the occasion and armed as scouts. An increase to the Kookie Levy would be a fitting reward to the men, many of whom would enlist, as well as being an advantage to ourselves.
15. The measure I would therefore prepare for the consideration of the Lieutt. Governor would be the increase of the Kooke Levy from 200 men to 640, duly officered by natives. And I would further recommend the appointment of an adjutant and two European non-commissioned officers, in addition to myself as Commandant, to insure the proper training and

discipline of the men. With such a force in Cachar when properly organised, the services of the Sylhet Light Infantry might be entirely dispensed with and made available for employment further West. And at the same time the District remain efficiently and chieply defended.

16. The pay of the Kookie Levy is at present rupees 5 per mensem. Moderate as this allowance is, it it sufficient to bring the required number of Kookies to the standard, but as it would be necessary to mix with the Kookies other races as well, in the proportion of at least one to three and as such good material as Goorkahs are at hand, to whom it would be necessary to offer an increased rate of pay, I think that 6 rupees a month would not be too much, and at that standard would I recommend the augmentation.

20th Feb., 1858

I have just been informed that another of the fugitive Munnipoorie Princes has escaped into Munnipoor, where the Rajah has people out for his apprehension. After one who is supposed to have fled into the Lhoochais Country, I have despatched a party of scouts with a view to warn the Lhoochais to give him up.

25th Feb., 1858

I have the honour to acknowledge the receipt of your letter of the 15th instant informing me of the apprehension of Howjou, a Munnipoorie Prince who broke his arrest at this place, and in reply request that you will cause the Rajah to have him sent to me as soon as it is convenient, in order that the object of his running away may be investigated.

27th Feb., 1858

1. ....this district is fast resuming its wonted quietness.
2. Three more mutineers of the 34th N. Infry were apprehended during the past week attempting to escape to the westward.

After some resistance they were captured by the villagers and have been tried and executed by me.

3. These last say that they formed part of a body of ten who escaped from the field of Binnacandy, and crossing the river entered the jungles on the opposite side. They have been they say, separated from the other seven for some time, and do not know whether they have been killed or not. As the place where these last three were captured renders it possible that their comrades have made for North Cachar, I have written to the officer in charge of that district to put him on his guard.

6th March, 1858

.... all is quiet in Cachar. One more mutineer was caught by the villagers a few days ago, endeavouring to make his way to the west.

13th March, 1858

.... there is nothing to relate with reference to any disturbances in Cachar. During the last week all remains quiet.

The above is repeated on March 20th, 27th, April 3rd, 10th, 17th & 24th.

10th May, 1858

1. .... Norindrojeet Sing, having been sent to Cachar by the Rajah of Munnipoor, I have tried him under Act XIV of 1857.
2. The evidence against him is most complete, even although he himself denies the charge of even having joined the mutineers at all. Three camp followers and six women belonging to the party of mutineers who were with them when the Munnipoories joined and who before Norindrojeet Sing's capture had described the man, although they did not know his name, recognised him at once; and besides

there were two Bengalees who were prisoners at the time in the camp of the mutineers. Doctor Shircore also deposes to having heard a sepoy of the 34th N. Infantry mention his name before execution, and describes the wound on his instep as a gun shot one, the Prince who joined being reported as wounded on the foot.

3. The defence set up by Norindrojeet Sing is that he was in the direction of Luckipoor when the disturbance commenced for the purpose of buying rice and that hearing that I wanted to confine him, he kept out of the way and eventually went to Munnipoor. The wound on his instep he describes as having been inflicted by a bamboo splinter and he summons witness, of whom only one can be found and that one denies all knowledge of anything cocerning him.
4. Although one of the witnesses expressly states that the purpose of Norindrojeet Sing was to take possession of Cachar, yet I do not think that his object was anything else but to secure the throne of Munnipoor, although it is possible that the conquest of Cachar may have been mooted in the mutineers' camp. In his excuse it has to be said that he is a very ignorant man and that his title to the throne of Munnipoor may be considered superior to that of the present occupant, Norindrojeet Sing being the son of an elder brother. He has moreover been forgiven by his cousin in power, who has, I believe, addressed the Supreme Government in his favour.
5. Taking these circumstances into consideration I am of the opinion that it would be inexpedient to sentence this prisoner capitally, and would recommend his confinement for life as a state prisoner.
6. I have taken the advantage of a large batch of prisoners proceeding to Calcutta under a strong guard and have forwarded Norindrojeet Sing along with them. His presence, and that of the other princes in Cachar, is not calculated to allay the excitement which has recently prevailed approve

of the step I have taken, instead of awaiting orders upon a reference.

7. The Princes, Howjou and Khocrapha, who escaped from jail in Cachar, where they were confined under suspicion, have also been tried. They cannot be found guilty of any specific offence except that of jail breaking, which they say they were induced to do from dread of the numerous executions which were then taking place. But their escape was so exactly timed with the junction of Norindrojeet and his party with the mutineers that I have little doubt that it was preconcerted. The Princes also accompany the guard proceeding with the convicts.

4th June, 1858

To

The Magistrate of the 24th Pergunnahs, Calcutta.

1. I have the honour to advise you of the despatch of a boat containing one Seikh Faqueer and twelve women and nine childern being the camp followers of the party of mutineers of the 34th N.I. who were hunted down in Cachar.
2. The Seikh Faqueer, who did some good service to Captain Dewal at Chittagung when the mutiny broke out has been pardoned, and is to be sent to his home. The women are also, by order of the government to be sent to their houses in as comfortable manner as possible.

In a letter written to the Secretary to the Government of Bengal on the 15th June, 1858, with reference to the troops stationed in Cachar, Stewart mentions that he does not think it essential that a European Force should be sent to the District. He however mentions that a petition was sent to the Governor-General from the Planters of Cachar praying for the protection of a party of English soldiers. He is entirely against the idea and mentions that there is no barrack accommodation for English troops and their supplies would also create a difficulty.

After this references to the Mutiny disappear from the records but on the 28th of February, 1859, there is a letter containing a reference to Kannai Sing, one of the Munnipoorie Princes who escaped from jail in January, 1858. He is described as a very dangerous character, and "I also lose no time in forwarding him Calcutta."

On the 11th of March he appears to have been successful in persuading the Government to rid Cachar of some of the Munnipoorie Princes and gives a list of eleven who had been despatched to Naddeah.

Annexure-2

Indian War of Independence 1857*

Part-I: The Volcano

Chapter-I

Swadharma & Swaraj

It is a simple truism patent even to the uneducated that the most tiny house cannot be built without a foundation strong enough to support its weight. When writers who profess to write the history of the Revolution that was enacted in India in 1857 ignore this common sense principle and do not try to discuss the real causes that led to it and impudently maintain that the vast edifice of the Revolution was built on a blade of straw, they must either be fools or, what is more probable, knaves. Anyway, it is certain that they are unfit for the holy work of the historian.

In all great religious and political revolutions, it is almost impossible to connect together links apparently inconsistent, without thoroughly understanding the principles which are at their root. On seeing a great work of machinery composed of innumerable screws and wheels doing work of tremendous magnitude if we do not understand how the power is produced, we may feel bewildering astonishment, but never the inner pleasure

*https://savorkar.org/en/pdfs/the_indian_war_of_independence_1857_with_publisgers_nose.v0001.pdf

due to knowledge. When writers describe such stirring events as the French Revolution or the religious revolution of Holland, the very splendour and magnitude of the crises they paint, often, dazzle and confuse their mind's eye and they rarely gather sufficient coolness and courage to go deep into the underlying principles. But without an exposition of the hidden causes and the mysterious forces that worked beneath, the essence of a revolution can never be made plain. And therefore it is that history attaches more importance to the exposition of principles than to mere narrative.

While searching after principles, historians often commit another mistake. For every act, there are various causes, direct and indirect, general and particular, accidental and necessary. In their proper classification lies the true skill of the historian. In this process of classification many historians get mixed up and make the accidental into a necessary cause. These make themselves as ridiculous as the judge in the story who, in a case of arson, put all the responsibility on the match instead of the man who struck it. The real importance of any event can never be understood by this confusion of causes. Not merely that, but mankind begins positively to curse the memory of men who are represented as having started, with a light heart and private selfish motives, a Revolution in the course of which countless lives are lost and immense expanses of country devastated. And therefore, in writing the history of any event in general, and of revolutionary movements in particular, a writer cannot give a true idea of them by means of simple description, or even by tracing them backwards to accidental causes. An upright and impartial historian must try to discover the foundations on which the revolutionary structure was erected. He must try to discover and discuss fundamental causes.

Mazzini, in a critical article on Carlyle's *French Revolution*, has said that every revolution must have had a fundamental principle. Revolution is a complete rearrangement in the life of historic man. A revolutionary movement cannot be based on a flimsy and momentary grievance. It is always due to some all-moving principle for which hundreds and thousands of men fight, before which thrones totter, crowns are destroyed and created, existing ideals are shattered and new ideals break forth, and for the sake of which vast masses of people think lightly of shedding sacred human blood. The moving spirits of revolutions are deemed holy or unholy in proportion as the principle underlying them is beneficial or wicked. As in private life, so also in history, the deeds of an individual or a nation are judged by the character of the motive. If we forget this test, we cannot appreciate the vast difference between the empire-building wars of Alexander the Great and Italy's fight for liberty under Garibaldi. Just as to decide about the merits of these two different events one has to consider the prime motive of the chief actors in those wars, so also to write a full history of a revolution means necessarily the tracing of all the events of that revolution back to their source—the motive, the innermost desire to those who brought it about. This is the telescope which will show clearly the lights and shadows obscured by the blurred presentation of partial and prejudiced historians. When a beginning is made in this manner, order appears in the apprent chaos of inconsistent facts, crooked lines become straight, and straight lines appear crooked, light appears where darkness is, and darkness spreads over light, what appeared ugly becomes fair and what looked beautiful is seen to be deformed. And expectedly, or unexpectedly, but in a clear form, the Revolution comes into the light of real history.

The history of the tremendous Revolution that was enacted in India in the year 1857 has never been written in this scientific spirit by any author, Indian or foreign. And hence there are current throughout the world most extraordinary, misleading, and unjust ideas about that Revolutionary War. English authors have committed, in this respect, all the faults noted above. Some of them have not made any attempt beyond merely describing the events, but most of them have written the history in a wicked and partial spirit. Their prejudiced eye could not or would not see the root principle of that Revolution. Is it possible, can any sane man maintain, that that all-embracing Revolution could have taken place without a principle to move it? Could that vast tidal wave from

Peshawar to Calcutta have risen in flood without a fixed intention of drowning something by means of its force? Could it be possible that the sieges of Delhi, the massacres of Cawnpore, the banner of the Empire, heroes dying for it, could it ever be possible that such noble and inspiring deeds have happened without a noble and inspiring end? Even a small village market does not take place without an end, a motive; how, then, can we believe that that great market opened and closed without any purpose—the great market whose shops were on every battlefield from Peshawar to Calcutta, where kingdoms and empires were being exchanged, and where the only current coin was blood? No, no. The market was neither opened nor closed without a purpose. English historians have always ignored this point, not because it is difficult to ascertain it, but because it is against their interests to admit the truth.

Even more deceptive than this indifference, and one which changes or distorts the whole spirit of the Revolution of 1857 is the other device of English historians copied by their Indian sycophants—the device, namely, of describing the rumour as to the greased cartridges as the moving cause of the Revolution. An Indian writer[1] drawing inspiration from English history and English money says, "Foolish people went mad simply at the rumour that cartridges were greased with cows' and pigs' fat. Did anyone inquire as to whether the report was true? One man said and another believed; because the second became disaffected, a third joined him, and so like a procession of blind men, a company of inconsiderate fools arose, and rebellion broke out." We propose to discuss later on whether people blindly believed the rumour about cartridges. But it will be plain to anyone who has read even the English historians closely and thought about the matter, that a great attempt has been made to father all the responsibility of the Revolution on this rumour. It is not surprising that to one, who thinks that a mighty rising like that of 1857 can be produced by such trifles, it was only 'a company of inconsiderate fools.' If the Revolution had been due only to the cartridges, why did Nana Sahib, the Emperor of Delhi,

1. शिपायांचे बंड–विनायक कोंडदेव ओक।

the Queen of Jhansi, and Khan Bahadur Khan of Rohilkhand join it? These were not surely going to serve in the English army, nor were they compelled to break the cartridges with their teeth! If the rising were due wholly or chiefly to the cartridges, it would have stopped suddenly as soon as the English Governor-General issued a proclamation that they should not be used any more! He gave them permission to make cartridges with their own hand. But instead of doing so, or ending the whole by leaving the Company's service altogether, the sepoys rose to fight in battle. Not only the sepoys but thousands of peaceful citizens and Rajas and Maharajas also rose, who had no direct or indirect connection with the army. It is therefore clear that it was not these accidental things that roused the spirit of the sepoy and the civilian, king and pauper, Hindu and Mahommedan.

Equally misleading is the theory that the rising was due to the annexation of Oudh. How many were fighting, taking their lives in their hands, that had no interest whatsoever in the fortunes of the Oudh dynasty? Then, what was their motive in fighting? The Nabob of Oudh himself was imprisoned in the fort of Calcutta; and according to the English historians, his subjects were very much disaffected under his regime. Then, why did Talukdars, soldiers, and almost every one of his subjects unsheath their swords for him? A 'Hindu' of Bengal wrote an essay in England at that time about the Revolution. In it the 'Hindu' says, "You have no idea how many simple and kind-hearted people who had never seen the Nabob, nor were ever again likely to see, wept in their huts when the sorrows of the Nabob were being related before them. And you do not also know how many soldiers were daily taking an oath, after the tears had flown, to avenge this insult on Wajid Ali Shah, as if a calamity had fallen on themselves in person." Why did the Sepoy feel this sympathy with the Nabob and why did eyes which had never seen the Nabob glisten with tears? It is plain, therefore, that the Revolution did not break out simply on account of the annexation of Oudh.

The fear of greased cartridges and the annexation of Oudh were only temporary and accidental causes. To turn these into real causes would never help us in understanding the real spirit of the Revolution. If we were to take them as the real moving causes, it would mean that, without these, the Revolution would not have taken placed—that without the rumour of greased cartridges and without the annexation of Outh, the Revolution would not have been there. It would be impossible to find a theory more foolish and more deceptive. If there had been no fear of the cartridges, the principle underlying that fear would have cropped up in some other form and produced a Revolution just the same. Even if Oudh had not been annexed, the principle of annexation would have manifested itself in the destruction of some other kingdom. The real causes of the French Revolution were not simply the high prices of grain, the Bastille, the King's leaving Paris, or the feasts. These might explain some incidents of the Revolution but not the Revolution as a whole. The kidnapping of Sita was only the incidental cause of the fight between Rama and Ravana. The real causes were deeper and more inward.

What, then, were the real causes and motives of this Revolution? What were they that they could make thousands of heroes unsheath their swords and flash them on the battlefield? What were they that they had the power to brighten up pale and rusty crowns and raise from the dust abased flags? What were they that for them men by the thousand willingly poured their blood year after year? What were they that Moulvies preached them, learned Brahmins blessed them, that for their success prayers went up to Heaven from the mosques of Delhi and the temples of Benares?

These great principles were *Swadharma* and *Swaraj*. In the thundering roar of 'Din, Din', which rose to protect religion, when there were evident signs of a cunning, dangerous, and destructive attack on religion dearer than life, and in the terrific blows dealt at the chain of slavery with the holy desire of acquiring *Swaraj*, when it was evident that chains of political slavery had been put round them and their God-given liberty wrested away by subtle tricks—in these two, lies the root-principle of the Revolutionary War. In what other history is the principle of love of one's religion and love of one's country manifested more nobly than in ours? However much foreign and partial historians might have tried to paint our glorious land in dark colours, so long as the name of Chitore has not been erased from the pages of our history, so long as the names of Pratapaditya and Guru Govind Singh are there, so long the principles of *Swadharma* and *Swaraj* will be embedded in the bone and marrow of all the sons of Hindusthan! They might be darkened for a time by the mist of slavery—even the sun has its clouds—but very soon the strong light of these self-same principles pierces through the mist and chases it away. Never before were there such a number of causes for the universal spreading of these traditional and noble principles as there were in 1857. These particular reasons revived most wonderfully the slightly unconscious feelings of Hindusthan, and the people began to prepare for the right for *Swadharma* and *Swaraj*. In his Proclamation of the establishment of *Swaraj*, the Emperor of Delhi says, "Oh, you sons of Hindusthan, if we make up our mind we can destroy the enemy in no time! We will destroy the enemy and will release from dread our religion and our country, dearer to us than life itself."[2] What is holier in this world than such a Revolutionary War, a war for the noble principles propounded in this sentence, "release from dead our religion and our country, dearer to us than life itself?" The seed of the Revolution of 1857 is in this holy and inspiring idea, clear and explicit, propounded from the throne of Delhi, THE PROTECTION OF RELIGION AND COUNTRY. In the Proclamation issued at Bareilly, he says "Hindus and Mahomedans of India! Arise! Brethren, arise! Of all the gifts of God, the most gracious is that of *Swaraj*. Will the oppressive Demon who has robbed us of it by deceit be able to keep it away from us for ever? Can such an act against the will of God stand for ever? No, no. The English have committed so many atrocities that the cup of their sins is already full. To add to it they have got now the wicked desire to destroy our holy religion! Are you going to

2. Leckey's *Fictitious Exposed* and Urdu works.

remain idle even now? God does not wish that you should remain so; for he has inspired in the hearts of Hindus and Mahomedans the desire to turn the English out of our country. And by the grace of God, and your valour, they will soon be so completely defeated that in this our Hindusthan there will not remain even the least trace of them! In this our army, the differences of small and great shall be forgotten, and equality shall be the rule; for, all who draw the sword in this holy war for the defence of religion are equally glorious. They are brethren, there is no rank among them. Therefore, I again say to all my Hindi brethren, "Arise and jump into battlefield for this divinely ordained and supreme duty!" The man who, after seeing such magnificent utterances by the Revolutionary leaders, does not understand its principles is, as we said, either a fool or a knave. What stronger evidence is needed to prove that Indian warriors drew their swords at the time for *Swadharma* and *Swaraj*, feeling it the duty of every man to fight for the rights given to man by God? These Proclamations issued at different times and placed during the war make it unnecessary to dilate more on its principles. These Proclamations were not issued by non-entities; but they were orders issued from adorable and powerful thrones. They were burning expressions of the agitated feelings of the time. In these the real heart of the Nation had spoken out, when at the time of war, there was no occasion to conceal real sentiments through pressure or fear. This trmendous, heroic shout, 'Swadharma and Swaraj', proclaims to the world the character of the Revolution in which 'all who draw the sword are equally glorious.'

But were these two principles understood as different and exclusive of each other? At least, orientals have never had the idea that *Swadharma* and *Swaraj* have no connection with each other. The Eastern mind has maintained a full and traditional belief, as is also said by Mazzini, that there is no vast barrier between Heaven and earth but that the two are ends of one and the same thing. Our idea of *Swadharma*, too, is not contradictory to that of *Swaraj*. The two are connected as means and end. *Swaraj* without *Swadharma* is despicable and *Swadharma* without *Swaraj* is powerless. The sword of material power, *Swaraj*, should always be ready drawn for our object, our safety is the other world, *Swadharma*. This trend of the Eastern mind will be often found in its history. The reason why, in the East all revolutions take a religious form, nay more, the reason why Eastern history knows of no revolutions unconnected with religion, lies in the all-embracing meaning that the word 'Dharma' has. That this dual principle of *Swadharma* and *Swaraj*, always seen in the history of India, appeared also in the Revolution of 1857, should be a matter of no surprise. We have already referred to the first Proclamation of the Emperor of Delhi. Afterwards when Delhi was beseiged by the English and the war was at its height, the Emperor issued another Proclamation addressing all Indians thus: "Why has God given us wealth, land, power? They are not for individual pleasure, but they are given for the holy object of defence of our religion." But where are now the means to attain this holy end? As said in the Proclamation given above, where is the gift of *Swaraj*, the greatest of all the gifts of God?

Where is wealth? Where is land? Where is power? In the plague of slavery, all this divine independence is all but dead. In the above Proclamation, in order to show how the plague of slavery was destroying India, full descriptions are given as to how the Kingdoms of Nagpur, Ayodhya, and Jhansi were trampled down into dust. And it awakens the people to the fact that they are guilty of the sin of destroying religion in the house of God, having lost these means of defending religion. The command of God is, Obtain *Swaraj*, for that is the chief key to the protection of *Dharma*. He who does not attempt to acquire *Swaraj*, he who sits silent in slavery, he is an atheist and hater of Religion. Therefore, rise for *Swadharma* and acquire *Swaraj*!

"Rise for *Swadharma* and acquire *Swaraj*!" What divine events in the history of India are due to the realisation of this prionciple! The poet-saint Ramdas gave the same dictum to the Mahrattas 250 years ago. "Die for your *Dharma*, kill the enemies of your *Dharma* while you are dying; in this way fight and kill, and take back your kingdom!"[3]

This alone is the principle in the Revolutionary War of 1857. This is its mental science. The true and clear form, is the above verse of Ramdas.

Seeing at it through this telescope, what a spectacle comes into view! The war fought for *Swadharma* does not lose its lustre by defeat. The splendour of Guru Govind Singh's life is none the less, because his efforts did not immediately succeed at the time. Nor do we think the less of the rising of 1848 in Italy, because the Revolution failed completely at that time.

Justin McCarthy says: "The fact was that throughout the greater part of the northern and north-western provinces of the Indian peninsula, there was a rebellion of the native races against the English power. It was not alone the Sepoy who rose in revolt – it was not by any means a merely military mutiny. It was a combination of military grievance, national hatred, and religious fanaticism against the English occupation of India. The native princes and the native soldiers were in it. The Mahomedan and the Hindu forgot their old religious antipathies to join against the Christian. Hatred and panic were the stimulants of that great rebellious movement. The quarrel about the greased cartridges was but the chance spark flung in among all the combustible material. If that spark had not lighted it, some other would have done the work .... *The Meerut Sepoys found, in a moment, a leader, a flag, and a cause, and the mutiny was transformed into a revolutionary war.* When they reached the Jumna, glittering in the morning light, they had all unconsciously seized one of the great critical moments of history and converted a military mutiny into a national and religious war! "[4]

Charles Ball writes: "At length, the torrent overflowed the banks, and saturated the moral soil of India. It was then expected that those waves would overwhelm and destroy the entire European element and that, when the torrent of rebellion should again confine itself within bounds, patriotic India, freed from its alien rulers,

---

3. धर्मासाठी मरावें। मरोनि अवघ्यास मारावें।
मारितां मारितां घ्यावें। राज्य आपुलें।

4. *History of Our Own Times*, Vol. III.

would bow only to the independent sceptre of a native price. The movement, now, assumed a more important aspect. It became the rebellion of a whole people incited to outrage by resentment for imaginary wrongs and sustained in their delusions by hatred and fanaticism."[5]

White writes in his *Complete History of the Great Sepoy War*: "I should be wanting in faithfulness as an historian if I failed to record with admiration the courage displayed by the Oudhians. The great fault of the Oudh Talukdars from a moral point of view was their having made a common cause with the murderous mutineers. But for this, they might have been regarded as noble patriots, fighting in a good cause, *pro rege et pro patria*, for the King and the Motherland"—for *Swaraj* and *Swadesh*!

Chapter II

The Chain of Causes

If it is true that the question whether India, bounded by the Himalayas on the north and the Ocean on the south, should be completely independent or not, was being solved on the battlefields of the war of 1857, then the chain of causes begins from that day in 1757 when the question was first raised. On the 23rd of June in 1757, the question whether India should belong to the Indians or to the English was openly discussed, for the first time, on the field of Plassey. On that very day and on that very field, where it was first discussed, were sown the seeds of the Revolution. If Plassey had not been there, the War of 1857 also would not have taken place. Though a century had rolled by, the memory of that day was fresh in the heart of Hindusthan. In proof of this, witness the terrible scene on the 23rd day of June 1857, in Northern India. In the vast country from the Punjab up to Calcutta, wherever there was an open field, thousands of Revolutionaries were fighting the English simultaneously in different places, from morning till evening, after

5. *Indian Mutiny*, Vol. I, p. 644.

openly challenging them saying: "To-day we are going to avenge Plassey!"

When, on the battlefield of Plassey, India had sworn to fight a war of freedom, England was, as it were, anxious to hasten the day of its fulfilment as much as possible. For, Englishmen did not rest with sowing the seeds of the Revolutionary War at Plassey, but they made enormous efforts to encourage the growth of the plant all over India. Warren Hastings tended the plant in Benares, Rohilkhand, and Bengal. Wellesley did the same in the fertile fields of Mysore, Assai, Poona, Satara, and Northern India. This was not done without strong efforts, for the ground had to be ploughed not with ordinary ploughs but with swords and guns! What would ordinary ploughs avail against Shanwar Palace, the heights of Sahyadri, the forts of Agra, and the throne of Delhi? When these rocky portions had been broken and crushed, the smaller pieces left out by mistake were also next broken. The smaller princes fell under the strokes of English perfidy, oppression, and tyranny.

The English did not even feed well or pat on the back the brutes by whose strength they effected all these conquests. For a hundred years, they had been oppressing and maltreating the sepoys in their army. When the soldiers of the Mahrattas or the Nizam won important victories, they used to get Jahgirs and rewards. But the Company gave nothing but 'sweet words' of praise. The sepoys, whose swords won India for the English, were so barbarously treated that General Arthur Wellesley would drive the wounded sepoys to the mouth of guns instead of sending them to the hospital!

While the English had thus been sowing the seeds of discontent and hatred in almost all parts of Hindusthan, the time soon came when it appeared that their efforts would soon be crowned with success. The danger to the independence of India was first perceived by Nana Farnavis of Poona and Hyder Sahib of Mysore. From that day onwards, the presence of this danger began to be seen, faintly at least, by the princes of India; and its effect was markedly seen in the "mutiny" at Vellore. This rising at Vellore was a rehearsal of the great rising of 1857. Just as in a theatre, before the actual performance, several rehearsals have to be gone through, so in history, before the actual and final attainment of freedom, in order to harmonise the whole performance, several rehearsals in the shape of risings are necessary. In Italy, the rehearsals started as early as 1821, and only in 1861 was the play successful. The Rising at Vellore in 1806 was such a rehearsal on a small scale. In this rising, the sepoys had been won over by the princes and people. At markets, preachers disguised as Fakirs were preaching. To indicate the time of rising, chapatees even had been distributed. Hindus and Mahomedans together had risen in the name of religion and liberty. But this being the first rehearsal, they fell even as they were rising. Never mind! Before the final performance, how many rehearsals have to be gone through! Only the actors should boldly stick to their tasks and never cease their rehearsals. And for producing this drama, both England and India were working day and night without rest. And those that were making ready to take part in the play were not common, poor, or ignorant folk. The Gadi of Tanjore, and Masnad of Mysore, the Raigarh of Sahyadri, the Dewan-I-Khas of Delhi were among the select actors. And to crown all, Lord Dalhousie landed on the shores of Hindusthan in 1846. There is not now much time left for commencing the task which was sworn to on the battlefield of Plassey.

From the above chain of causes, it will be clearly seen that, before Dalhousie landed in India, the seeds of discontent had gone deep, very dedep, all over Hindusthan. Rajas and Maharajas, deprived of their kingdoms by the English, were burning in their hearts. The fact that the centenary of Plassey was approaching inspired a strange feeling of hope among the people; and in the very armies of the English, the sepoys were secretly chafing with rage and hatred. Even if India had had at this time a Viceroy who would strive to allay this secret discontent, it is very doubtful how far his efforts would have been successful. The question now was not whether the Company's rule should be good or bad; but the only question that used to be asked all over the country was whether the rule should exist at all. The one other force that was necessary for making an attempt to solve definitely this question was supplied when Dalhousie became viceroy; for he gave up the policy of coating poison pills with sugar before administering them to the victim, and began a system of open and direct oppression which did not fail to burn its way into the hearts of the masses.

Lord Dalhousie is described, by English historians, as one of the founders of the English Empire. This fact alone is sufficient to form an estimate of his capacity and character. In a country where unjust wars of conquest and oppression of foreign nationalities and races are universally popular, it is no wonder that those who have committed the greatest injustice and oppression are the most honoured. Thus, he who is most unjust is deemed the most capable, and one has no better way of proving himself a great man in such a country than by committing a climax of injustice. In such an Empire, where there is such an emulation of injustice and oppression, Lord Dalhousie was given the significant title of a 'founder'; it is impossible to find a more suitable word to describe his character. With the result of a hundred years of wicked English policy behind him, obstinate by nature, possessed of boundless self-confident, his flesh and blood permitted by the glory and pride of an unjust Empire, this bold, if not clever, man landed on the shores of out land saying openly, "I will level the land of Hindusthan."

As soon as Dalhousie landed, he saw at once that so long as Ranjit Singh's lions lived in the Panjab, it was impossible to achieve, the object dear to his heart of levelling Hindusthan. He, therefore, determined to throw somehow or other the lion of the Panjab in the cage of Slavery. But the Panjab lion had no ordinary claws. Seeing his cave threatened, he rushed out of the lair at Chillianwalla and, with a terrible stroke of his paw, mauled the enemy and made him bleed. But, alas! While the lion was standing at the mouth of the cave at Chillianwalla, a traitor broke open the back-wall at Guzerat and the lion was surprised and captured. Soon the cave of the lion became his cage! Ranjit's Queen, Chand Kuvar, dies rotting in London! And the lion's cub, Dhulip Singh, ate the beggar's bread at the hands of the Feringhi enemy!

After the annexation of the Panjab, Lord Dalhousie wrote in his despatch, the proud sentence that the extent of the British Empire was now continuous from the Himalayas to Cape Comorin. But now that the British frontiers had been pushed to the Himalayas on the north and to the seas on the south, it was inevitable that he should have an ambition to create an eastern and a western frontier suitable to these northern and southern ones. Then why delay? Send a 'peace' mission to Burma and the work is done. This peace mission so tightly embraced the peace of Burma that its ribs were broken and it expired! This very loving task was soon over and Burma was also annexed. Now at last, the whole of Hindusthan – from the Himalayas to Rameshwaram and from the Sindhu to the Iravady became red—but, oh! Dalhousie , do you not fear that it will soon be redder still?

Do we realise what is meant by the annexation of the Panjab and Burma? We cannot form an idea of it from mere names. The Panjab alone is a territory of 50,000 sq. miles and a population of four millions! It is the land watered by five sacred rivers of the Vedas, on the banks of which the *Rishis* in ancient times had recited sacred *mantras*! To conquer such a region Alexander came from Greece, to defend such a region King Porus fought. After taking such a country, the ambition even of Ravana would have been satisfied; but the land-hunger of Dalhousie was not satisfied even after swallowing not only the Panjab but also the extensive dominion of Burma. Though the frontiers of India were extended, there still remained the graves of ancient kingdoms within. Dalhousie therefore began to root these out and level everything. Not only did they occupy too much valuable space, but there was the fear that from these graves might one day rise the future avengers of India's wrongs.

In the grave at Satara was buried a magnificent Hindu Empire. And it is no wonder that Dalhousie, who was a believer in the Resurrection of Jesus was afraid that out of Satara might rise a future Hindu Emperor who would confound the foreigner and establish *Swaraj*. In April 1848, Appa Sahib, the Maharaja of Satara, died. At this news, Dalhousie decided to annex that State. And what was the reason? The king had no direct heirs! Even the cottage of the village labourer who has no direct heir is not confiscated but is given to his adopted son or to his near relatives. And Satara was not a peasant's cottage but an 'ally' of the English Government. In the year 1839, Pratap Singh Chhatrapati had been charged with having engaged in a conspiracy with the object of overthrowing the British Government, was dethroned, and in his place Chhatrapati Appa Sahib was appointed by the English Sirkar to succeed him.[1] Mr. Arnold, in his book *Dalhousie's Administration*, says, "It is not pleasant to dwell, on the circumstances of the dethronement – so discreditable they were." After such shamelessly discreditable dethronement, the English established on the Gadi of Satara the brother, on account of the failure of legitimate sons. By this, the English practically acknowledged the right of other relations – as is the invariable law laid down by the Hindu Shastras – to succeed to the throne. The only truth about this whole affair is that Dalhousie, with the habitual treachery of his nation, overrode this open acknowledgement knowingly and deliberately, because it was profitable to do so.

No one could under any pretext say that the English in any of the various treaties concluded with the various Rajas, had refused to acknowledge the right of adopted children to succeed to their adoptive parents' thrones. In 1825, the Company, while acknowledging the right of the adopted child of the Raja of Kota to succeed, openly declared: "*The Prince of Kota must be considered to possess the right, in common with all other Hindus, of adopting a son and successor in conformity with the rules of the Shastras.*"

---

1. The first article in the treaty entered into by the Sirkar with the Chhatrapati, when he was placed on the throne of Satara, runs as follows: "The valiant English Government on its part agrees to give the country or territory specified, to the Government or State of His Highness the Maharaja Chhatrapati (the Raja of Satara); His Highness the Maharaja Chhatrapati and His Highness's sons and heirs and successors are perpetually, that is from generation to generation, to reign in sovereignty over the said territory."

Again, in 1837, when the Raja of Oorcha adopted a successor, the English acknowledged him and promised:

> "Hindu sovereigns have a right to adopt, to the exclusion of collateral heirs, and the British Government is bound to acknowledge the adoption, provided it is regular and not in violation of the Hindu law."[2] It may be safely asserted that nowhere else but in English politics could be found the audacity of denying the very existence of those promises which were given most definitely and which are contained in their own documents. Not only by these declarations but on innumerable other occasions, the English have acknowledged the right of the native princes to adopt in accordance with the Hindu Shastras. Suffice it to say that, within the short period of two years (1846-47), the English Government had consented to the succession to the Gadi of innumerable adopted sons, and acknowledged their rights.

Indeed, to try to seek, in the language of promises and treaties, the root cause of annexing these states, is to work in a wrong direction altogether. The real truth of the matter is that Dalhousie had come to reduce all India to a dead level and the grave of the Hindu Empire at Sarata was trying to raise its head. Obviously, therefore, though Pratap Singh and Appa Sahib had both adopted in accordance with the Hindu Shastras, the English annexed the Raj under the pretext of failure to legitimate heirs. The Gadi of Satara! The same Gadi on which Shivaji was crowned by the hand of Gaga Bhatt! The same Gadi to which Baji Rao I dedicated all his triumph, before which he bowed low! O Maharashtra! behold that same Gadi, on which Shivaji sat, and to which homage was paid by Santaji, Dhanaji, Niraji, and Baji, has been broken to pieces by Dalhousie! Go on, if you will, with your petitions and deputations. What if Dalhousie does not listen to these? In England at least, you

---

2. *Parliamentary Papers*, 15th February, 1850, p. 141.

think, the Directors will listen to you? Dalhousie is apparently a mere man; but, who knows, perhaps the Directors in England might be more than men. None in Maharashtra has seen these same Gods. It was, therefore, thought proper that Rango Bapuji, an excellent and loyal man, should go to England to lay the grievances of Satara before the 'Home' authorities. Success or no success, the game was at least, they thought, worth trying. But how long would they wait, hoping against hope, for the success of their mission? For how long would Rango Bapuji go on wearing away the very pavement of Leadenhall Street? Yes, Rango Bapuji will go on clinging to his impossible hope till he is mocked at and insulted, till every penny is spent in feeding English barristers with crores of Rupees so that he has not money left even for his passage, and until he receives the insolent reply that they refuse to give back Satara!

While Rango Bapuji was busy packing for London, Dalhousie's attention was being absorbed by a new affair; for, an occasion had risen by which he could weed out the miserable shrunken shrub of the *Raj* of Nagpur. Raghoji Bhonsle, the rightful owner of the Nagpur Gadi, died suddenly at the age of 47. The Raja of Berar was an ally of the Engliosh Government[3], and this very friendship of the English was the cause of his destruction! Those who knew that the English hated them were spared but all those who foolishly believed that the English were their friends were mercilessly and treacherously involved in ruin. The kingdom of the Berars was not the Englishman's *jahgir*, nor was it a feudatory state dependent for its existence on his sweet will and pleasure. It was an independent state on an equality with the Feringhi Sirkar. J. Sylvian has defied the British Government to show on what grounds and by what show of justice, either eastern or western, they could have the right of annexing such a *Raj*, merely because the king died childless. Obviously it was a game of legerdemain or sleight-of-hand; one removes and the other, his accomplice, conceals it quietly! While

---

3. The treaty of 1826 beging as follows: Treaty of perpetual friendship between the Honourable East India Company and His Highness of Maharaja Raghoji Bhonsle, his heirs and successors.

the one cuts off the head, the other, his accomplice, goes on asking loudly by what law he dared commit the deed—as if murderers and highway robbers need the law to back them up. In 1853, then Dalhousie at last laid his murderous knife at the throat of 'his friend', showing as a reason that the Raja had not adopted a successor. Raja Raghoji had every hope of a child but died suddenly. Even if he died without a child, the right of adopting passed at his death to his legal wife. If the English had not acknowledged at any time previously the heirs adopted by the queens of deceased Rajas, we should have had nothing to say. But it remains a fact that the English had acknowledged the adoption of Daulatrao Scindia's widow in 1826, the adoption by Junkoji Scindia's widow in 1836, the adoption by the widow of the Raja of Dhar in 1834, and the adoption by the queen of Kishengarh in 1841. Not one, not two, but many such adoptions have the English acknowledged. But we should not forget the fact that, on these occasions, it was to their advantage to acknowledge these heirs. In this case, on the other hand, it was not to their advantage to acknowledge the adoption by the widow of Raghoji. The real point at issue, then was one of advantage to the English Government, and everything was determined on that issue. While the Raj of Nagpur was annexed because no adoption took place, the Satara kingdom faced a similar fate because the adopted heir should have a right to succeed to the throne! Impossible for logic to step in here.

By annexing Nagpur, Dalhousie robbed an extensive tract of 76,832 sq. miles, with a population of 46,50,000 people and an enormous annual income. While the poor Ranees were weeping themselves hoarse, a loud knock came on the palace gate. The door was opened and in rushed the English troops. Horses were let loose from the stables, elephants—after forcibly pulling down the Ranees riding on them—were taken to the bazaars for sale, and silver and gold ornaments were removed from the palace and were sold by public auction in every street. The necklace that adorned a queen was lying in the dust of the bazaars. Elephants were sold for 100 Rupees! After this you will hardly be surprised to learn that horses, fed on richer food than Dalhousie had for his own dinners, were sold for 20 Rupees and that a pair of horses, on which the Raja himself used to ride, was sold for 5 Rupees! Elephants with the *howdas* on them and horses with caparisons were sold, but the Ranees still remained with their jewels. Why not sell the jewels? So, the jewels also went the way of other things, and no Ranee had a single jewel left on her person. But even here the "friendship" of the English could not stop. So, they began to dig the floor of the palace! And, Heavens, in the very bedroom of the Ranees the Feringhi pickaxe began its desecrating work! Reader, start not yet, not tremble, for the pickaxe has only started the work, and will do further deeds, nay, is doing it. For, see you not it has broken the bedstead of the Queen, and is digging the very flooring underneath the bed? And shall we say it? All the while the Maharanee Anna Poorna Bai was on her death-bed, and was even then dying! While the Dowager Queen of the great family of the Bhonsles of Nagpur was on her deathbed, groaning with agony and for the insult to the throne and the family, in the neighbouring room, in that bed of the Queen, the Feringhi's pickaxe was doing its work! What a terrible accompaniment to the groans in the next room! And why all this? Because Raghoji died before adopting a successor!

Ranee Anna Poorna Bai died, groaning for the insufferable insults flung at her ancient dynasty. But the hope of Ranee Banka to get justice from England was not yet dead! This vain hope was at last destroyed, but not until she had tried the immensely expensive remedy of feeing English barristers with lakhs of Rupees. And what did Ranee Banka do then? She spent the rest of her life in "loyalty" to the Feringhi! While the Lightning was working destruction at Jhansi, Banka, seeing that her sons were ready to unsheath their swords of *Swaraj*, threatened them that, if they did unsheath their swords, she would herself inform the Feringhis of their designs and advise the Feringhis to behead them!

Index